THE SUN STILL
RISES

Hope & Healing in the Wake of Genocide

SARAH SUTHERLAND

www.ten16press.com - Waukesha, WI

For information, please contact:

www.ten16press.com
Waukesha, WI

Cover design by Kaeley Dunteman
Copy Editor: Samantha Jacquest

The author has made every effort to ensure that the information within this book was accurate at the time of publication. The author does not assume and hereby disclaims any liability to any party for any loss, damage, or disruption caused by errors or omissions, whether such errors or omissions result from accident, negligence, or any other cause.

All photographs were taken in Rwanda. Please note that not all images are correlated with the regions represented in each chapter.

The true authors are those who have told their stories: Teta, Scholastique, Antoine, Clement, Elyse, Yvette, Mary Jane, Innocent, Alphonse, and Fabian. I cannot thank you enough for sharing your pain, your strength, your hope, and your healing with all who read this. Your lives have the power to change our deeply divided world. Thank you for trusting me enough to share your stories.

PREFACE

My interest in Rwanda began in 2012 when I was an undergraduate elementary education major at the University of Wisconsin-Madison. As a student teacher, I worked under a cooperating teacher, Mika Oriedo, and taught middle school-aged children about the 1994 genocide of the Tutsi in Rwanda. My godfather, Steve Mayer, had visited Rwanda numerous times and he brought his good friend Ben Kayumba, a Rwandan who was visiting the United States, to Sennett Middle School to speak to our students. While visiting the school, Ben recounted to staff and students how he had survived the genocide. His narrative heightened my interest in the country, and his suggestion to teach in Rwanda prompted me to apply for international teaching positions. A few months after meeting Ben in the United States, I graduated from college, packed my bags, and embarked on my journey as a first-year teacher in rural Rwanda from 2012 to 2013, where I taught English at an all-girls secondary school.

I could never have anticipated all I was about to learn.

In addition to teaching, I worked with Ben for a nonprofit organization called Good News International. Ben founded this nonprofit in an effort to alleviate the material poverty and to heal the emotional and spiritual wounds of his fellow genocide survivors. I traveled with Ben and other Good News staff, visiting communities across the country. Community leaders informed us of progress and expressed urgent needs, and the survivors shared their personal testimonies. Young adults spoke about how they had rebuilt their lives without the support of parents, siblings, or extended family members. Elderly women shared how they had continued to live without their husbands and children. Many stories included not only the trauma of the past, but also gratitude for the present and hope for the future. The physical, emotional, and spiritual resilience of these individuals was incomprehensible.

As I lived nestled safely within the hills of Rwanda, I was lovingly accepted into the lives of strangers who became dear friends. In time, I was gradually given the opportunity to see beyond the surface smiles and friendly hugs. When I arrived in Rwanda, I could not comprehend the beauty of the country, nor could my mind align the tranquility of the people with the eyewitness accounts of the past I would soon hear.

As I came to know the people of Rwanda, I learned that many had overcome significant hardship to achieve their present success. I learned the university graduate was a sole survivor of his family, the woman studying for her master's degree barely escaped with her life, and a woman whose beautiful voice joyfully sang praises unto God had lost six siblings, including her twin, and her parents. I desperately searched to find the keys that unlocked the buoyancy and resilience of life within these stories of redemption. While the previous requirements of publicly identifying ethnicities had been eliminated, the cultural bloodbath that occurred will never be erased from the memories of the survivors.

After living and teaching in Rwanda, I returned to the United States to wrestle with a multitude of questions that arose as I processed all I had witnessed. I decided to document the testimonies of those who survived the genocide of the Tutsi in Rwanda in an effort to comprehend and share the forgiveness and hope they had cultivated in their lives. When I returned to Rwanda in July of 2014 for a short trip, I interviewed young adults who had been children during the genocide. I conducted all interviews with the following guiding principles in mind:

- A person is more than his or her pain.
- A person's mental and emotional health is more important than his or her story.
- These are their stories to be shared as they want them to be told (the idea here was to, as objectively as possible, not shape my questions through the lens of my western perceptions so as to not influence responses).
- Healing is possible.
- Listen and learn.

All of the interviewees were between the ages of five and fifteen during the genocide, and are representative of a generation of silenced children who witnessed the horrors of the atrocities committed in Rwanda in 1994.

The majority of the interviewees in this book are people I know personally. I have visited their homes and met their families and friends. We have shared countless hours, conversations, and meals with one another. It was only as our relationships developed that I slowly learned about the trauma they experienced. It has only been twenty-six years since the genocide, and Rwandans still carry the trauma with them. The survivors who were children at the time have grown up in a post-genocide world with new difficulties and unwritten rules than the generations before them. I encouraged interviewees to share not only their experiences of having survived the genocide, but also the lives they've built in the aftermath.

For some participants, this was their first experience telling their complete life narratives.

While recounting these histories was obviously distressing, I was committed to protecting the emotional state of the individuals who agreed to participate, and did not press them beyond their limits. Interviewees were not prodded to recount traumatic experiences in depth.

Participants were assured that their story would be recounted as they told it. Some people were fluent in English and chose to speak in English. Others alternated between English and Kinyarwanda, and therefore parts of their narratives were translated. Others spoke only in Kinyarwanda and their stories were interpreted into English by a staff member from Good News International, named Clement. Clement has worked for Good News since it's foundation, and participated in genocide survivor relief programs as a child and young adult. His personal story of survival and life post-genocide is also included in the following chapters. All oral interviews were first recorded, later transcribed, and finally, lightly edited for comprehension. Three interviewees participated via a written questionnaire.

While this is not the case for all Rwandans, I intentionally chose people who had experienced significant spiritual and emotional healing for two reasons: It was more likely they would be able to tell their stories with limited emotional harm, and to learn *how* this healing was possible. At the end of each narrative, interviewees were asked to share a lesson they had learned through their life experiences that they wanted to teach others.

UNDERSTANDING RWANDA:
A HISTORICAL CONTEXT

In order to understand survivors' accounts of the genocide, it is critical to understand Rwanda's history. The intensity and severity of the genocide varied regionally, thus greatly impacting individual experiences during 1994.

Prior to colonization, many different clans populated the region that is now Rwanda. In addition to identifying by clan, individuals also identified by class. The Tutsis were the upper-class, and their wealth was marked by owning and herding cattle. The Hutus were the lower-class who cultivated the land. An individual's identification as Hutu or Tutsi was fluid as an individual gained or lost wealth. As the wealthier class, the Tutsis developed an aristocracy and peacefully ruled the region.

Germans first visited the court of the Tutsi king in 1894. In the wake of the king's death in 1897, the Germans claimed the land that is now Rwanda and Burundi and ruled it as one colony named Ruanda-Urundi. Germany was able to gain control of the land due to the dispute that ensued among the Tutsi people, as to who the deceased king's successor would be. Germany indirectly ruled through the Tutsi aristocracy until World War I when Belgium assumed control of the colony.

Belgian colonizers maintained the Tutsi aristocracy, and continued the Tutsi-Hutu class distinction to preserve Belgian power through indirect rule. In 1933, Belgian colonizers developed a system that converted the fluid Tutsi-Hutu social class distinction into rigid ethnicities. Those with more than ten cows were registered as Tutsi, and those with less than ten cows were registered as Hutu. About eighty-five percent of the population was registered as Hutu and fourteen percent as Tutsi. The final one percent of the population was registered as Twa, who had Pygmy origins, and were the original indigenous peoples to the region. Belgian colonizers issued identity cards that solidified the newly created ethnicities. This act forever altered the Tutsi-Hutu distinction. The Belgians' continued exercise of oppressive colonial power over the Tutsis bred Hutu resentment, and planted the seed for future ethnic violence.

In the late 1950s, Hutus first revolted against the Tutsi aristocracy. Tutsis maintained power, and ethnic tensions intensified. Rwanda gained independence from Belgium in 1962. Without Belgian support, the aristocracy collapsed and 120,000 Tutsis fled the country. The shift in power paved the way for Grégoire Kayibanda, leader of the Party for Hutu Emancipation, to win the first presidential elections.

Ethnic tensions and violence continued in Rwanda over the next three decades. Hutus maintained governmental control and Tutsi refugees were not allowed back into the country. Tutsi refugees outside the country organized attacks in an effort to regain Tutsi power within Rwanda. These attacks led to increased discrimination of Tutsis within Rwanda, more Tutsis fleeing the country as refugees, and retaliation killings of Tutsi civilians. Violence peaked in 1963 when Tutsi guerillas from neighboring countries attacked, and the Hutus-controlled government responded by killing an estimated fourteen thousand Tutsis civilians living in southern Rwanda.

Juvénal Habyarimana replaced Grégoire Kayibanda as president in 1973. President Habyarimana remained in power for the next twenty-one years. By the end of the 1980s, nearly half a million Tutsis lived as refugees in neighboring East African countries and were forbidden to return to Rwanda. Tutsi exiles in Uganda formed the Rwandan Patriotic Front (RPF) in 1990, a rebel army committed to ending President Habyarimana's regime.

From 1990 to 1994 discrimination of Tutsis within Rwanda intensified. Hutu extremists created and published a document named "The Hutu Ten Commandments," propaganda that spread the ideology of Hutu supremacy to the general population. The government organized youth militia called the Interahamwe, which means "those who attack together." The Interahamwe were indoctrinated with the ideology of Hutu supremacy, and trained to use machetes. The government, in conjunction with the Interahamwe, created regional lists of locations of Tutsi households.

In 1992 and 1993, President Habyarimana engaged in peace talks with the RPF. The president signed treaties that included a ceasefire, gave the RPF representation as a political party within Rwanda, and allowed for the reintegration of Tutsi refugees. Ultimately, the goal of these treaties was to shift the country to a transitional government. The United Nations established the United Nations Assistance Mission in Rwanda (UNAMIR) to ensure the stipulations of the treaties were enacted peacefully. Hutu extremists were angered by these treaties, and responded by increasing discrimination and violence against Tutsi civilians.

On the night of April 6, 1994, an airplane carrying the presidents of Rwanda and Burundi was shot down by a missile, and both presidents were killed. Immediately, Hutu extremist leaders accused the RPF of the assassination, and called the Interahamwe to lead Hutu civilians to end the "Tutsi problem" once and for all. After years of Hutu Power propaganda, training of Interahamwe militia, and curating a list of Tutsi households across the country, the death of Rwandan president Habyarimana was the spark Hutu extremists needed to launch the country into genocide. To this day, the origin of the missile's site and the party responsible is unknown.

On the morning of April 7, 1994, radio stations notified the nation of President Habyarimana's death. Radio announcers called civilians to arms within their communities to "cut the tall grass" and exterminate the "cockroaches" and "Tutsi snakes." Led by the Hutu-dominated government and the Interahamwe militia, former friends and family members picked up machetes and the butchering began. In some parts of the country the Interahamwe set up roadblocks within hours of the president's death. Anyone who passed was required to show their identity card. Hutus were allowed to continue, while Tutsis were murdered on the roadside. Later that day, the Hutu prime minister and the ten Belgian peacekeepers protecting her were killed by Interahamwe. After their deaths, Belgium lobbied other foreign nations to reduce UNAMIR peacekeepers in Rwanda from 2,165 down to 270. The absence of international intervention allowed for years of planning, preparation, and genocide ideology to be executed as Hutus slaughtered their fellow Tutsi community members.

The next one hundred days were a nightmare of unimaginable horrors as women and girls were victims of gruesome acts of sexual violence, innocent children were mercilessly slaughtered, and Tutsis were hunted down by their Hutu neighbors. The majestic, emerald hills of Rwanda were bathed in blood and littered with mutilated bodies. A country whose beauty constitutes an earthly paradise was transformed into the bowels of hell. The world's inaction came at the cost of over one million lives, with the deepest wounds left on those who witnessed these atrocities and survived to be forever haunted by the memories.

The mass number of perpetrators, the violent methods of murder, and the communal relationships between victims and perpetrators, have left uniquely devastating scars on the Rwandan people.[1]

---

[1] All of the information found in this chapter was gathered from articles on HistoryWorld.net and the United Nations website:
http://www.historyworld.net/wrldhis/PlainTextHistories.asp?historyid=ad24
https://www.un.org/en/preventgenocide/rwanda/historical-background.shtml

INTRODUCTION

Amid the clamor of the crowd, I look to my cooperating teacher, Mika Oriedo, as I attempt to hide my uneasiness. He smiles and affirmatively shakes his head, understanding my unspoken reservations. "It's all you, Steach," he says.

I take a deep breath, stand up, and briskly step to the front of the auditorium. I turn to face more than one hundred middle school students, striving to mask my nerves under a false sense of confidence. My ability (or inability, as the case may be) to silence the din of the large group will soon be revealed. I quickly bury my anxiety and inhale while raising my hand, signaling, and saying, "In five...four...three..."

An inaudible sigh of relief escapes my lips and the room comes to a hush once I get to zero, allowing me to introduce our guest speaker Ben Kayumba, founder of the nonprofit Good News International, and survivor of the 1994 genocide of the Tutsi in Rwanda. I'm proud of the speaker I've arranged to make history come alive for our students. Ben is a good friend of my godfather, Steve Mayer, who has facilitated Ben's visit to Sennett Middle School, where I am doing my student teaching. After weeks of teaching about the genocide of the Tutsi in Rwanda to middle school students, I settle into my seat with eager anticipation, mindful of the honor it is to have a genocide survivor here in our school.

My attention quickly moves from the students and my role as a student teacher, and focuses toward the front of the auditorium. Learning about the horrors of the Tutsi genocide alongside my cooperating teacher and middle school students was one thing, but hearing, seeing, and meeting Ben, a survivor of this tragedy was completely another.

I am transported beyond the Sennett Middle School odors, wood folding seats, cramped bodies, and life as I know it as Ben delivers his harrowing narrative of death, disguise, risk, and escape. Being snuck out of Rwanda by a taxi driver who would later be murdered for aiding in his rescue; running across the border, then continuing to run, to hide; realizing a previous phone call was the last time he'd hear the voice of his beloved fiancé. Returning after the genocide to discover his home had been burned to the ground, and in the ground were the bodies of his parents, siblings, and relatives.

I am deeply moved by Ben's story as I visualize my parents, siblings, relatives, and dear friends murdered. I cannot come close to imagining such heartache and loss.

What did he just say? His childhood *friend* murdered his family? Later in his life, he encountered this man and forgave him?

Currently living in Rwanda with his wife and four children, Ben now devotes his life to supporting fellow survivors, especially the orphans and widows—the most vulnerable—who still live under dire conditions. He encourages survivors to forgive those who murdered their families.

I am hearing words that are beyond my capacity to comprehend. Forgiving former friends and neighbors who became rapists and murderers? Unconsciously shaking my head, incredulous, I snap back to reality as the narrative turns and twists to its place in the present.

I clap along with an unusually attentive and hushed middle school audience. With their teachers, the students file out of the auditorium to their respective classrooms. I slip to the front to thank Ben for coming to speak to the students.

"Thank you so much," I say, as I extend my hand and smile, knowing my words will never adequately express the gratitude I feel.

My head reels. The firsthand account of the Tutsi genocide I've just heard transmutes into the reality of his strong handshake and warm, brown eyes.

"Murakoze," Ben replies with a smile. *Thank you.*

I introduce myself and answer his questions about my upcoming graduation and uncertain future. When Ben learns I do not yet have a teaching job for the fall, he suggests I come teach in Rwanda. For the first time, I find myself considering the idea. Although it seems implausible to plan a year abroad in only two months, my determination brings a sense of peace; teaching abroad in the tiny country of Rwanda is suddenly at the forefront of my mind. Ben senses my interest, and immediately offers to help find a school where I can teach, and we exchange contact information.

Suddenly I realize the students have almost filtered out, and I am reminded of my student teacher responsibilities. I say my goodbyes to Ben. Little do I know that soon we will meet again, and next time, I will be the foreigner.

Three months later, the time finally came for me to pack my bags, and move to Rwanda as a teacher.

One ocean, twenty-four hours, many countries, and two planes later I arrive, wheels finally touching down in my final destination. My tired arms hoist the mini library in my carry-on down from the overhead bin. The heat of excitement burns away questions that threaten to creep in and distract my mind from being fully present. I take eager steps. What will await me?

My feet come to rest on the tarmac, firmly planted. I breathe prayers of gratitude as I look to the sky, close my eyes, and drink in the rich air that fills my nostrils and lungs. Following the passengers now flowing freely around me, I walk into a small room, dimly lit, and stand in line for customs. I step to the desk, fumble around in my bags and through my purse, and hand over my passport. The custom official eyes me up, down, and up again, then stamps my passport, and says, "Okay." I am motioned to move forward with the flick of a hand and eyes that move beyond me to the next person.

The other weary travelers and I shuffle to baggage claim. Exhausted yet determined, I teeter with my hiking pack, backpack, and two rolling suitcases. One year's worth of living essentials are condensed on my back and wheeled by my hands. Turning the corner, I am deluged by a sea of unknown faces and waves of unfamiliar language. Some people hold signs with names written on them. Searching the crowd, suddenly the situation dawns on me-will I recognize Ben? Will he recognize me? What if he's not…? Caught in mid-thought, all questions are extinguished as his deep eyes and strong, kind smile appear. He embraces me in arms clothed in a Green Bay Packer jacket. "Karibu. Murakaza neza." Welcome.

Stepping back from the embrace, I see two shy Rwandans behind Ben, who move forward to welcome me with smiles and hugs. Clement and Scholastique introduce themselves, and I learn they work with Ben at Good News International, an organization dedicated to providing relief to genocide survivors.

All my luggage is taken off my hands before I can protest. Ben chats casually as we head to his truck; conversation shifts fluidly between English and Kinyarwanda. I consume every sight, every sound, every smell. My senses are on fire as I beg my mind to etch each moment into memory, determined never to forget the ups, downs, and bends of the hills of Kigali. People walk, bike, drive; horns honk, motorcycles weave, movement everywhere. Mental images solidify into snapshots that I carefully tuck into preciously guarded alcoves, a reserve for cherished memories that intersect at my mind and heart. Strands of my hair fly loose and swirl in the night around me, as the sweet, rich Rwandan breeze caresses my face. Breathing in the nighttime air, I bottle the smell in a vial of memory to be forever treasured. I am tingling with life.

CHAPTER 1:
TETA, SCHOLASTIQUE, ANTOINE

Region: Kigali

In the capital city of Kigali in April of 2013, I elbow my way through packed streets and push my way onto overcrowded buses. As my skin touches and sweat mingles with those around me, I cannot help but wonder about the Rwandan people. I ponder the relationship of the person on my right to the one on my left, noting the scars peeking out of the sleeves of one, but not the other. Winding through the maze of the marketplace, my senses are overwhelmed by sights, sounds, and smells. Shouts of the lowest prices and the freshest fruits and vegetables, colors flashing, eyes darting, old wounds covering the arms of the woman in the third stall, yet not in the fourth. A turning head and brightly wrapped hair highlighting pale lines crisscrossing along the back of the neck of an elderly vendor. An older man hacking meat off a cow's carcass in the stalls lining the sides of the market. All working alongside each other, striving for survival. I marvel at the interplay of their lives in the present as I contemplate how their lives may have intersected in the past.

Kigali has been the capital city of Rwanda since its independence in 1962, and is heralded across Africa for its cleanliness, organization, and advancement. While the city and architecture expand, decades-old mass graves from the genocide continue to be uncovered.

The capital wasn't always a city of progress, however. Just an hour after the president's plane was shot down on April 6, 1994, roadblocks were erected across Kigali to check the ethnicity of all who passed by. As the center of Hutu Power, Tutsis living in Kigali were in extreme danger. Seen as the center of the government of Rwanda, the Rwandan army and the RPF used the limited modern weapons they had access to, and battled for control of the city. Within Kigali, Amahoro stadium became one of the few safe havens for Tutsis. As the genocide continued and the fighting within Kigali between the Rwandan army and the RPF continued, the stadium became increasingly unsafe.[2]

Scholastique is a survivor who was at Amahoro for part of the genocide that lasted from April to July 1994. Teta and Antoine are also from Kigali and were in different areas of the city as they fled the killers. Scholastique is a staff member of Good News International, Teta is a Good News community member who sells clothing to make a living, and Antoine is a staff member of the Christian organization Youth with a Mission.

---

[2] https://www.hrw.org/reports/1999/rwanda/Geno15-8-01.htm

1: Teta Florence

Name: Teta Florence
Year and place of birth: 1979, Gikondo, Kigali
Age during genocide: fifteen
Family members killed during genocide: parents, twin, and five other brothers and sisters
Family members who survived genocide: none
Schooling completed: senior three [American equivalent of ninth grade]
Occupation: sells clothes at market
Currently lives with: lives alone
Language spoken for interview: Kinyarwanda; interpreted into English by Clement Ndayisaba

I look tentatively over to Clement, as he pauses while interpreting Teta's story. His eyes tell me it's okay; stay quiet and let her speak—or not speak. I take his unspoken advice, sit still, and silently pray for comfort to reach across the expanse and touch the depths of her scars. In the silence, I am overcome with empathy of the pain that is evident in Teta's face. She pauses, takes a deep breath. She continues. Pauses again, her eyes fill, unable to stop the overflow. She can't speak, continues to take deep breaths as tears roll down her cheeks. I get tissues and quietly pass them to Teta. Birds chirp, the sun shines, tears roll, and words surface from the depths. She continues, touching upon agonizing details. Her eyes close as the images of precious, innocent, mutilated bodies fill her mind and become words that escape the confines of her memory. Silently, I listen, wishing it wasn't true. She pauses. Silence. The rustling of leaves. The symphony of melodies from the branches. Breathing. She continues.

We lived in Gikondo, Kigali before the genocide. My father was a pastor, and we had a good family. We had cows, and we had a good amount of wealth. My father had a small car, which helped us economically. We were a close family and we enjoyed our lives. We were all Christians, and we went to a Pentecostal church. I was the third born of the seven children, and I had a twin.

I first learned about ethnic groups in 1990 when people came to my home. They would come and sometimes take my brother, and once they took my father. We asked where they were taking them, and they said they were taking them away because they were Tutsis. They took my older brother into the forest near our house, stripped him of clothes, and started beating him. When he came home in the evening, he was in a bad condition, and was sick and injured for a whole month. That's how my siblings and I first learned about the ethnic groups. When they took my father, we didn't know where they brought him. [Evidently] they took [him] to prison for two and a half months. We didn't know the details of what happened while he was there, although we knew he wasn't well treated.

During that time, my parents didn't let us children know everything that was happening because they were trying to protect us. However, people in our community were accusing my family of holding meetings in our home [for] Inkotanyi (RPF) because people knew that one of my cousins went to join the RPF [The RPF was the Tutsi-led army that fought against the Hutu-led government at the time]. The community around my home was mixed ethnically, but most of the people were Tutsi and many of them were killed.

The people who currently live in that area came from other places. At that time Tutsis dominated that area of Gikondo.

I remember that two days before the genocide started, on April 5, many people came to our home. We had two houses, and one was used for a prayer group. On April 5, many people came to pray. Many of those people were in our family, but there were also neighbors and friends. All of them were Tutsi, and when they came they told us that God showed them that something bad was going to happen, and that God told them to pray about it every day. During the night of April 6, we heard that the president's plane crashed and that he died. When we woke up on the morning of April 7, before we ate breakfast, we saw a lot of movement all around. Some people were shouting, others were being beaten, and we didn't know what was happening. We tried to go out of our house as a family, but when we went out we saw many people starting to surround our house. We thought that they were coming to our house to do something bad. My father ordered us to go to the other door of the house, and he stayed with my uncle and they started to go towards the people to talk to them. They wanted to ask what was happening and what they wanted, but before they could ask they took my uncle, and killed him immediately. When my father saw this, he immediately ran away. After my father ran away, they came into the house, started killing our cows, taking the meat, and taking the property from our house. After the house was empty, they started destroying the house itself, and killing people they found in the area. We couldn't go back home, and so we started living in the sorghum bushes where we would sleep during the night. I was with my mom, and all of my younger brothers and sister[s]. My older sister was not with us, because she was married and she was pregnant. My older brother was also in a different area.

We were living in the sorghum bushes, and we couldn't leave there during the day because people might find us. We decided to move in the night, so no one could see us. My twin and I were very hungry, and it was raining. My family decided to try to go and find my older sister, who was married and lived with her own family. When we were on the way toward where she lived, we found her dead body. We found that she had been killed, and tortured in a horrible way. They had taken a big stick, and put it up her vagina all the way up to her neck. She had been pregnant with twins, and before they killed her, they cut open her stomach, and pulled the babies out of her. My whole family was together when we found my older sister like this, and we saw that they had tortured her. My father took the stick out of her body, and my mother took her *igitenge* [African cloth] to cover the bodies of my sister and her twins. We were not able to give my sister and her babies a proper burial, because people were chasing us to kill us. We were forced to immediately leave, and so we left them there.

After we left them, it was evening, and so we went back to the sorghum bushes. It was [the] rainy season, and my brothers and sisters and I were so hungry because it had been a long time since we had had food. We were only drinking water. When it rained we made a small hole in the soil, and put grass over the top to filter the water. So when it rained, we would drink that water. It was about four days since [we] had food, and so my mother asked my father to go out and see if he could find a potato or cassava field to bring one to us children, because she was afraid we would die of hunger. My father planned to wait until the evening to find food. But my mother saw we were very hungry and going to die, so she decided to go immediately to the neighbors to find food. But when she left the sorghum bushes, many people saw her and started shouting, "These are Inkotanyi! These are Tutsis!" They ran to her and began killing her. She was near where we were hiding, and so we saw them catch her, and start to cut her with the machetes. She was shouting, "God please receive me! God please receive me! God please receive me!" and after she yelled that, she died.

When they were killing her, my father took all of us together, and he was praying for us. I remember my father praying for us, and he told us to be patient, that we would soon meet our mother in heaven, because that is where we were also going to be. But he begged that anyone who survived, if anyone survived, should be a hero and survive to live a better life. He held me in his hands and said, "God is showing me that one of you will survive, and you will do better things [than] we did before."

When they first saw my mother, they saw the bush where she had come from. After they had killed her, they entered the bush where we were, and started killing us. They started with my father. They were killing him with the machete, and cutting him on his head. However, there were many killers, and so some of them had also started killing my brothers and sisters. They beat me on the head with a big stick, and I was lying on the ground like a dead person. Because of this, they thought that we had all died. Once they thought we were all dead, the killers immediately left us.

I don't know how much time passed, but eventually I woke up, although I didn't remember what happened because I was traumatized. When I tried to move, I felt my hands touching someone. I looked around and saw it was my father. Because I didn't remember what happened, I asked him to give me water because I was so thirsty, even though he was already dead. On the other side of me were my brothers and sisters, and they were all dead. I also had been cut by machetes and was laying in blood. I couldn't move. I was touching the bodies of my family members all around me, and eventually I remembered what had happened. I stayed there with their bodies for two days, and I thought I would also die.

After two days the RPF came into the area, and although there were many dead bodies lying around, they saw me moving and realized I was still alive. So they came and immediately took me to King Faisal Hospital in Kigali to be treated. I stayed there for a long time, because I had so many physical wounds all over my body. Since I laid there for two days without any treatment, I also had many issues that had developed inside my body. I was treated with different medications, and I saw many doctors. It was not easy for me to get healed, and so I stayed there for a long time. I don't remember how long I was there, but I know it was a long time. During that time in the hospital the main problem I had was with my leg that had been cut with machetes. I couldn't stand, and I could only sit. They gave me medication, and after some time they started to teach me how to stand and walk again. They would have me stand for one minute, then sit. And slowly they increased the amount of time I could stand. I was also given crutches to help me start moving properly.

After I was healed, they took me to an orphanage in Rugunga, where I stayed for three years. After three years, the orphanage was giving children to families who wanted to adopt them. When [we] were at the orphanage we went to church on Sundays to meet other children in Sunday school. One of the other orphans I lived with had a good friend in the Sunday school, and the friend decided to come and take her. When she came, she decided to take both of us to her family. I was about eighteen at the time I was adopted.

At that time, I wasn't thinking anything about God, because I spent my time thinking about the pain of my physical wounds and about my family. I always remembered how they were killed. However, I didn't share with anyone about what happened to me in the genocide and about my family, but instead I just kept quiet. People would ask me why I was so quiet and why I didn't talk very much.

We were not actually adopted into the family by the parents, but it was the older children that took us from the orphanage to live with them. When we got there we were happy to be there, and we had peace with them. We loved them and they loved us. After we had stayed with the family for some time, we realized that the parents had been killers during the genocide. When the RPF came in the country, the family had fled to Congo with many of the other killers. After some time, they came back from Congo to Rwanda. The father had killed so many people. In the back of the house, there was a big hole with the bodies of many people who were killed. At first, we didn't realize that the hole had been used for this purpose. He also had a list of people in his house who were supposed to be killed.

He soon realized that we were old enough to understand what the papers were about, and what he had done. After the father returned to the house, within one month he asked us to leave, and told us he didn't want us to live there.

This was a big point of change in my life; because I had nowhere to live, I would go here and there, and sleep here and there, but I didn't have a place to live. I think [I] was around twenty years old at that time, although it's not easy to remember everything that happened during that time.

At that time all my physical wounds had healed, but now I struggled to have a place to sleep and food to eat. Life was not easy. I went to pray with people in churches, and I joined a choir. My strategy was to find people who had prayer groups during the night, so that I could stay with them overnight, because I didn't have a place to sleep. I was not happy. I questioned God all the time. I only joined these groups to have a place to sleep at night.

I remember one time when I was hungry, I went to see [a different] friend and their family. It was lunchtime, so I shared lunch with them. I had a small plastic bag that I used to keep and carry my clothes. After eating, I asked the family for some water so that I could wash my body and my clothes, and change my clothes. After I washed, I went aside and started asking God, "Why did you let me survive? What is your purpose for my life?" I was so angry with God during this time. After I had washed, they invited me to stay overnight with them. I was so grateful for the opportunity.

That night, while I was sleeping, I had a dream. It was the image of [a] man, and the man reminded me of a president. In my dream, he came near me, where I was sleeping, and he said, "Teta, I know you and I know everything that you went through; I know every step of your life. I will never leave you. I am with you, and I am staying with you. Don't worry about everything that you are going through. You will serve me and you will do everything to fulfill the purpose that I have for your life." Then I immediately woke up, and I knew that it was God who had spoken to me.

They next morning I immediately went to church and I found my pastor. I told him about my dream, and he told me he also believed it was the voice of the real God speaking to me. I asked the pastor to allow me to spend my time in the church and stay there, and he said that I could do that. I didn't tell the pastor that I wanted to sleep there, but I decided on my own that I would do that. I came in the evening to sleep there, and left early in the morning so no one would know that I was sleeping there. During the days I would go back to where my home used to be and I would stay there, then during the evenings I would go back to the church. However, the watchman saw me every morning, and after one week he called the pastor and told him I was staying there. He asked the pastor to come early one morning to talk to me.

The next day, when I woke up around 5:00 a.m., I saw a car. I tried to pass the car, but I saw it was the pastor. He stopped me and called me over to him. He told me that he knew I was staying in the church at night, but that this was the first he knew of it. He asked how he could help me, and how he could pray for me. I wasn't able to respond to him-I started weeping. He opened the car door and took me to his home. The pastor gave me breakfast, but I was not able to eat because I wasn't feeling well. He asked me again where I had been staying during the days, but I couldn't tell him.

After that he took me to a place in Kigali near Kacyiru, and paid rent for a house for three months. They gave me food, materials for the house, and everything basic for life that I would need. This is how I began living on my own. This is how life started for me. I started going to church, joining groups, and thinking about what I could do to support myself. I don't remember how old I was at this time, but I was not more than twenty-five.

I thought about how I could survive, and I was able to find some jobs. I went to places to ask for cleaning jobs, washed clothes, and got trainings from hotels about the tourist industry. I used to move all around to find a job. Sometimes I would find a job for three months or more, and when the job was finished, I would search until I found another one.

I took steps personally when I met with other people who had similar testimonies that I did. When I met with people and we shared what happened to our families during the genocide, I received comfort from them and from the word of God they shared with me. This is when I started to feel spiritual comfort which forms the foundation of the life I have today.

There are things I have learned from my life experiences that I would like to share with others. When all the ways are closed, where can you go? When all the foundations are broken, what do you have left? When everyone and everything is gone, who can you trust and what do you base your life on? In my life, I had no one but God. He is the only one who will be there for us when we have no one and when we are left with nothing. I know there are some people who have many struggles. It may not be genocide, but people have had challenges that have touched their lives. I want them to know that there is a God. No matter what the situation is, no matter what happens, there is a God, and God cares for His people.

Even though I went through different challenges, there was a time when I was able to comfort others. I was inspired by God to comfort others and tell them God was with them. No matter what you have been through, God is using you to touch others. When you approach people who are down and comfort them and lift them, God is always with you to support you.

Stay near God. Wait for his promises. God always gives promises, but we don't want to wait for them. We say we want things now, and if we don't get them, we leave. But that is not how God works. I learned that God is different than people. What we feel God should do is different than what he does. Sometimes we feel like we are not with God, but He's working in other ways, and He is always with us. God will never leave us. In anything and everything that happens, God is always with us. He does things in a better way than we would do them, although sometimes we do not realize that at the time. Sometimes when I want to ask God for things, I ask Him to do it His way, and I ask to be able to see Him working in my life. We have to wait for God's timing, because he is always planning better things for our lives than we could plan for ourselves.

II: Scholastique Uwantege

Name: Scholastique Uwantege
Year and place of birth: 1987, Remera, Kigali
Age during genocide: six
Family members killed during genocide: father and twenty-five extended family members
Family members who survived genocide: mother, three siblings, five aunts from mother's side, two aunts from father's side
Schooling completed: master's degree in accounting
Occupation: accountant for Good News Guesthouse and Good News International, owner of a children's clothing boutique
Currently lives with: her husband Elyse and two children
Language spoken for interview: Kinyarwanda and English; portions spoken in Kinyarwanda interpreted into English by Clement Ndayisaba

"Sarah, you know I never have done this," she begins.

I reassure her. I will ask questions, but I won't ask too many, and she doesn't have to answer anything she doesn't want to.

"I will do it for you. I want people to know," she confidently insists.

Before genocide, I was very young. I can't say that I knew much of what was happening, but of course, I remember things that I saw with my own eyes. I remember when my mother had conversations with my dad, and when they talked about the bad things that were happening to my father. Sometimes, people would come to take my father, but I didn't know who took him or why they were taking him. There was one time when my dad came home and he had been beaten so badly that he could no longer see out of [one eye]. We were not aware of how bad they were, and that they wanted to kill him. After that time, he started talking more openly about how bad these men were. My mom would tell him he needed to come home early because sometimes he came late in the night. My mom wanted him to come home before it was dark. He used to be an artist, but after his eye was destroyed he could no longer do this. He drank beer and was a tough man. He was not afraid of the men who beat him, and he felt like no one could really cause him trouble. I clearly remember one lady who sold beer. She always planned with other people to do bad things to my father. She would call him to come and drink at her place, to trap him. We started realizing how dangerous it was, and so my dad started coming home earlier. We were not allowed to leave the house or be out after 6:00 p.m. We knew that people had made a list of all the Tutsis, and that we were supposed to be killed. There was a group of Tutsis that my father was in that met to plan ways to protect themselves and their families, so that we would not be killed. He used to go to these meetings, but when he came back he would not tell my mom about what they talked about because he didn't want her to be afraid.

Before the genocide started, my mom's sister had married a Hutu man. Because my dad knew the genocide was going to start soon, he took all of us to that family. Since the man was Hutu, my father knew we would be safe there. Even though I was still young, I was the oldest of the children. At that time, I had a younger brother and a younger sister, and my mother was pregnant. My parents sent us children to my aunt and uncle's house, but my parents stayed at our house. They sent us to their house the day before the genocide started. We got there safely and stayed there. After we arrived, we heard that things were changing and getting very bad. My aunt and uncle took us to the roof of the house, to hide us there. When they were taking us up to the roof, my young brother started crying and asking what was going on, because he was too young to understand what was happening. My uncle came in to tell him to be quiet and was strict with him. Although he was tough on my brother, he did it in a loving way because if he continued to make noise, we would all have been killed. When my brother was crying, they took him and hid him under the bed with my aunt so that he didn't come up on the roof. My uncle was able to go out and get information about what was going on. He brought food to us up on the roof and to my auntie and brother under the bed. During that time, we wondered if my parents were still alive. However, God was with us, and he kept us protected. We stayed there for three days.

Even though people may be brothers and sisters, born from the same parents, they can be different. Some can have good hearts, while others do not. When we were hiding there, my uncle was protecting us and caring for us, but his brothers were bad people. His brother kept saying that he knew we were hiding there. He ordered my uncle to kick us out and threatened that he would bring people to the house to kill us.

When he was threatening my uncle during the genocide, he didn't know where my parents were. He left my uncle's house that day to go and look for my father. He immediately left and went to my parents' house. When he got there, my parents were hiding near the window to try to hear what was going on outside. When the man got there, he didn't go alone. He had also gone with three other Interahamwe killers. He was leading, and the others followed behind him. They had traditional weapons, including machetes and sticks. He didn't realize that my dad knew we were at my auntie's. He was yelling to my father and saying that he wanted us, the children.

He pretended like he was going to help my father and lied, saying he wanted to bring us, the children, to our uncle and auntie to be protected. My mom and dad listened to him yelling for them, but they stayed hiding. He continued to yell for my parents but because my parents were hiding near the window, they saw that he was with Interahamwe killers, and they all had weapons. He knocked on the door and circled around the house. He pretended to be alone and was trying to trick them, which is why he continued knocking. Since my dad saw him, my parents realized that he was lying, and they stayed quiet. He searched around the outside of the house for my parents, but since he didn't find them and they didn't answer the door, he thought that they had already left.

[That] brother of my [uncle's] is still alive, and I recently saw him. When he sees us, he is ashamed because of what he did during the genocide. I asked my mother why he was still alive and free, and why he was not in prison. People knew what he had done during the genocide, including what he had done to my family. My mother doesn't like it when I think about him or talk about him. I always think about this man during the genocide-remembrance time. My mom tells me that we are saved by the Lord and that we shouldn't do anything bad to him. She says that his conscience troubles him for what he has done and that we should just let him struggle with what he's done and not do anything negative to him. My mother says we need to leave him, because he's probably done bad things to others. Maybe he will be condemned by others and not us.

That's how I know, that even if people who are brothers, they can be totally different. One brother protected us, while the other brother was a killer. He never even came to us after the genocide to repent and ask for forgiveness. [Genocide perpetrators asking for forgiveness was a common occurrence in Gacaca courts— community gatherings where killers could opt to come forward, confess their crimes, and ask for forgiveness. Many people who committed murder never went to prison or were tried by the judicial system in Rwanda, due to the sheer number of perpetrators and the system's inability to handle this volume of people.]

He's still alive, but doesn't join our family in weddings or holidays. He is ashamed of what he did. Less than a year ago, these brothers lost their father, and my mom went to support the family. I wondered why my mom would go to support a man who had tried to kill us. My mother prays that I can be healed and forgive him for what he has done. Even though he is a bad man, she tells me that I cannot act badly toward him. Among my siblings, I was the oldest and I knew everything he did. My brothers and sisters don't know everything this man has done. I know that he knows I remember everything, because every time he meets my mom, he asks why I don't greet him or go to visit him. But he also doesn't greet me. I have never forgiven him because he has never asked for forgiveness. He was someone who could have protected us, yet he wanted to kill us.

After three days at my auntie's, they announced that all Tutsis should be taken to Amahoro National Stadium, so that's where we went. The stadium was a five-minute walk from where we lived. My auntie's husband stayed at the house, and we went with my auntie to the stadium because she was also in danger. When we were walking to the stadium, we had taken food from my auntie's. We had taken a small container of beans. I was carrying the container on my head; one hand was holding my sister's hand, and the other hand was holding my brother's hand. I also had a bag on my back. We were slowly moving like this, when all of the sudden, a grenade landed nearby. I was so surprised and the beans fell off my head. I always remember that image when we were moving toward the stadium. I think about what it feels like to be a refugee trying to move with everything. That image is so clear in my memory.

When we got to the stadium, we found my dad and mom, although I don't know how they got there or how they received communication to go to the stadium. But when we got there, we found them there. I don't know if you know what happened in the parliament, but there was an argument between the former government and the RPF before President Habyarimana was killed. Before my mom and dad got to the stadium, they already had many troubles. There was shooting, grenades being thrown between the parliament and the RPF soldiers. My parents had to travel through this fighting to get to the stadium. There were many times where they should have been killed. Miraculously, they both made it to the stadium and we met there.

I cannot fully express how awful it was in the stadium. It was the first time I had seen people dying. You could be standing next to someone, and a grenade was thrown and their head would blow off, and they would die next to you. Because the stadium was full of people, it was difficult to know how and when everyone was being killed. Sometimes people would sleep next to you, and because of all the grenades thrown in the stadium, in the morning you would find the body totally destroyed by the grenades, and the person next to you dead.

When the Interahamwe thought that most of the Tutsis from the area were in the stadium, they decided that we should all be killed. When we were living in the stadium, we were given biscuits by the UN peacekeeping soldiers. Most of them were from Ghana and Senegal. They helped protect all of us in the stadium. I still sometimes eat the kind of biscuits the soldiers gave us. We stayed in the stadium about three weeks.

Because my dad was tough and always trying to find ways to protect us, he joined a group of men at the stadium who worked to protect the people in the stadium. I'm not sure how the group of men my father was strategizing with got their information, but they found out that in Byumba, in northern Rwanda, the war was already over. After we learned that, there was a man who was our neighbor who had a big, blue truck. He took some people from his family and my whole family in his truck. He was a Tutsi man and had brought his truck into the stadium. However, my dad stayed in the stadium. After we left the stadium toward Byumba, I don't exactly remember the problems we dealt with along the way, but I remember that we were stopped many times and people tried to kill us. Some of the people with us were bribing the soldiers with money to let us continue alive. Because there were so many of us, we all laid down in the back of the truck. I don't know how many people were there, but it was as many people as could fit in the back of the truck. We were squeezed, because we took as many people as possible with us. We were all laying on top of each other.

Since I don't remember much that happened on the way, I've asked my mom what happened during that time. She doesn't want to talk about it and doesn't like that I think about it. She feels that thinking about the genocide will cause me trouble, so she wants me to spend my time thinking about other things. When you asked me about sharing my testimony, I went back to my mom to ask her some questions. Since she would not answer my questions, I went to my auntie. My auntie shared with me some information, but at a certain point she also asked me to stop asking questions and to leave the topic alone.

[Traditional Rwandan culture maintains an air of privacy and secrecy. Emotions are not publicly shown, and there are not systems in place for counseling or therapy. The older generations in Rwanda often do not want to speak of the genocide, and feel it's best to keep moving forward and not dwell on the past.]

When we got to Byumba, the RPF was in control of the area, so the genocide had stopped there. When we got there, we ate wheat as bread or porridge. Other people also came and gave us some clothes. In other parts of the country, however, the genocide was still going on. I don't know what happened to my dad during that time, because we left him at the stadium. We thought he had already died, but when we came back from Byumba, we found him alive. I don't remember how long we were there, but it was a long time. We got to know the area and made friends our age who we played with.

I don't remember exactly when my youngest sister Aline was born, but it was during the genocide. My father did everything to protect my mother during the genocide, because she was close to giving birth. When we were in Byumba, I remember my mother was ready to give birth. She couldn't move or do things quickly. My mother is a big woman, and so no one realized how pregnant she was. People started to realize because she wasn't able to do many things. Aline was born when we were on the way from Byumba back to Kigali, near the end of the genocide. [My mother] didn't go to the hospital to deliver, but her friends helped her deliver. When Aline misbehaves, my mother tells her how difficult it was when she was born. Aline also asks my mom many questions about the genocide, but my mom doesn't reply. My mother doesn't want Aline to have the problems that she would have if she knew everything that had happened.

When we came back to Kigali, the genocide had ended. We came back to our home area, but didn't go back to our original house. We stayed in another house nearby. We started learning that many people were killed, [and] how they were killed. We learned how my grandmother was killed. They killed her in a bad way and had taken off all of her clothing. We were able to recover her body and bury her in the Gisozi memorial site in Kigali. My grandfather had already died in 1959, when they had done a smaller genocide. Discrimination had been happening all over the country for many years, because my auntie shared how they used to beat her and yelled at her when she walked to and from school. She was beat everyday going to school. That's how we realized what had happened in the past, and how it connected to the genocide.

Because I was interested in knowing how my father's family was killed, I went to ask what had happened. What I learned was that besides my grandmother, we did not know how anyone on my dad's side was killed, and we were not able to bury any of them. Recently, on the twentieth genocide anniversary in 2014, we received some information about one of them. I learned from my auntie that my grandma, my father's mother, was killed in Kayumba forest. She was cut with machetes and was buried alive. There is a compound with beekeepers, where they buried most of the people. I asked my auntie if the bees were stinging them while they were tortured, but my auntie said she didn't know and asked me to stop asking questions. I went to the site, and we found many clothes of those who had died. There were so many people who died there, so we could not identify which body was my grandma's. My aunt really struggles with the fact that she has never been able to find their bodies and give them a proper burial. Because they lived near Nyamata, we believe they were killed near there. We go to the Nyamata memorial site to honor them and recognize their lives.

My auntie also told me about someone named Uwagatera, my dad's younger brother. I didn't know him, but she told me that after they killed him, they threw him in a pit latrine. My auntie also told me of another older relative who lived near that place [who] was also thrown in the latrines. She also told me about [aunt of mine] who was killed with her five kids in a similar way. Her husband was also killed and thrown into a water tank. These are the only relatives [that] she knew how they were killed, and then she asked me to stop asking her questions. We were not able to find them or bury them, but we know they are in heaven and are in peace. She also told me about another relative who looked like my brother. We never had any information about where, or if, he was killed. We wonder if he's still alive and living in another country.

My father was someone who was known as a Tutsi, because

he was always standing up for justice. One year after the genocide, my father was riding his motorbike. He was riding in Kigali, near Kanombe and the military camp there. There was a man—I don't know if he's Hutu or Tutsi—that saw everything and told us what happened. There was a car with soldiers in it that was following my father. The car that was following him hit my father on his motorbike. To make sure he was dead, they went back, and continued to roll over him with the car. We didn't get any more information about those men or that car. Even though there was security within the country, there [were] still many Interahamwe killing people in the country. At first, we didn't know where my father was and why he didn't come back home. We went to the prisons to look for him, and although we couldn't get any information about him, we didn't think that he had died. The man who saw everything happen took him to the hospital after the accident, but it was too late. After that he came to find us and tell us that he had been killed. After my father died, we lived in terrible conditions.

During that time there was so much mistrust among people and there was hate and anger. We were living a terrible life and it's hard to fully describe how awful it was. We were lucky to be paid by FARG, a government program that gave relief to survivors. Normally, FARG paid tuition for secondary school, but because our situation was so bad, they paid for our primary school as well. We are lucky that we always had the opportunity to go to school. My mom really struggled to find food and find other basic things we needed, but I praise God because we never had to go overnight without any food. God provided for us every day. My mom didn't have any school degree and couldn't get a professional job. She worked hard and got loans from the bank to provide for our family.

I thank God for how He was with us throughout this time. Spiritually, my family was not part of any church before the genocide. My mom became a Christian after the genocide. She went to church to seek God and to try to find peace. During that time, my mother kept pushing us to come to church with her. When I was about fourteen years old, I started going to church and following her to pray every Sunday. After I started going to church, I hadn't yet received Jesus, but I started singing in the choir and I loved it. During that time, I was very quiet and shy. People wondered why I was like that, but I stayed quiet so that I would not misbehave or disappoint my mom. In senior two [eighth grade], they were sharing the word of God. That's when I realized that no one could save me or release me, aside from Jesus. I started weeping and opened my heart for Jesus to come in and clean everything in my heart. When I fully received Jesus as the savior of my life, I started my journey of spiritual healing.

During the genocide remembrance time, I still feel sad, and there is a heaviness on my heart that's hard to express. I want to go far away from people and not talk or listen to anyone. I was young during the genocide, but now my mind relives the things that happened during that time. However, now I thank God for where we are today. I am proud of myself and my family, because we are able to help others and contribute to their lives. We must praise the Lord for what He's done for us.

Currently, my mom is still creating jobs and finding work to do. She never gives up and always encourages me when I am discouraged. She believes we can achieve. The house we are living in now was in an area that was totally destroyed during the genocide. My mom has built a new house on land where her parents used to live. Her family was killed on that land during the genocide, and now she is rebuilding life there. She moved into that house in 2013. We are proud to see the place remade after the total destruction of the killers. We never thought we would move back to Karembure, but we made it back there because my mom is a hero. I thank her, because she has never begged for anything. She continued to work and take out loans until she could pay them back. She has a loan now, but she's working and paying the bank back. We have a saying in Kinyarwanda, that says when children are young, they will go in the kitchen and fall down and have problems. Now my mother tells us that we are no longer little children. Once she repays this loan, I will not allow her to take out any more loans. Now, I am able to support her, to have her daily needs met, and to start [a small] business. I am so proud of her, and so thankful for all that she has done.

The message I want to share with people is to not focus on the past, but to look forward and see what is coming. I know the killers don't want us to go ahead and move forward in life; they want us to stay behind and struggle. It's not easy to move forward, but it is possible to be encouraged and think and plan for the future. We cannot stay tied in the sorrow of the past. I encourage you to look ahead, no matter what problem you may be facing. Even in Rwanda, there are messages that the survivors' children [are] misbehaving and not performing in class. Some people act that way because of all they went through, but it should not be like this. We should still be examples for our society. Another lesson is to work together in unity. People need to have common objectives and to work together to meet them. You need to have people you trust to help you with your problems. We must feel confident in ourselves and trust others enough to share our stories and our problems.

III: Antoine Umuhire

Name: Antoine Umuhire
Year and place of birth: 1983, Nyarugenge, Kigali
Age during genocide: eleven
Family members killed during genocide: mother, two younger brothers, and many other relatives
Family members who survived genocide: father, sister, two uncles, three aunts, some cousins
Schooling completed: Diploma in Alternative Energy from Tumba College of Technology [American equivalent of a bachelors' degree]
Occupation: missionary with Youth with a Mission (YWAM) in Kigali
Currently lives with: wife
Language spoken for interview: English

"What will you write?" he asks me.

"Whatever you say," I reply with a smile.

We stroll around the grounds and through the garden of the YWAM where Antoine lives and works. We find a shady seat to escape the blistering sunshine. I explain the process of the interview, ask him his language preference, and show him the audio recorder. In form true to Rwandan culture, he is a generous host and once he is sure I'm comfortable, bringing me a soda to sip while we talk, I feel irony and shame yet again. I should be making sure he is comfortable, physically and emotionally, before I ask him to launch into the narrative of his past and, unavoidably, into agonizing pain.

Giving me permission to record, we begin.

Graciously, he allows me to interject with clarifying questions, and answers them to ensure my understanding. I do my best to catch each detail. I observe his frame amid the garden surrounding us, knowing the audio recorder I hold can never capture the weariness in his eyes, the strength of his being, or the spirit of his faith.

I was born in a family of four children, and I was the second born after my sister. My mother was a tailor and made clothes. My dad did different jobs, but never had one stable job. Some days he worked in the bar, other days he sold spare parts. My father was a brilliant student, but because of his tribe, they didn't allow him to continue school. My dad came into Kigali in 1979 from Kibuye in the western province and he went back to bring my mom from there as well.

I was born in 1983, but my life was not good. Life was hard because I had two younger brothers and I had a health issue when I was young. When I was five years old, I began to see things in my community that I didn't understand. Both in my community and at school, people would ask me what my tribe was. I didn't know what I was, but they told me I was Tutsi, so I said what they told me to say, and I would answer their questions without thinking. My parents never told me I was Tutsi or talked about tribes, but from living with others in my community, I learned I was Tutsi, others were Hutu, and others were Twa. I sometimes saw people fighting, but I didn't understand why things were like that.

When I was five, things became very bad in my family. My dad had an issue with alcoholism, and he would drink a lot and not control himself. Life was not good because of my dad's alcoholism. I don't know how his drinking started because I had heard he was not like that before, but all I saw was him beating my mom, and we sometimes spent the nights outside of the house because of him.

It was hard to understand what was going on, and why my life was like that. I asked, "Why me?" but then I had to accept that was how things were, and that was my life.

I started school and was doing well in my studies, but I didn't take school seriously. I started to join other kids in the community who were getting into trouble. I started drinking, going to the cinema, and watching violent films and porn at a very young age. My friends and I started acting out the lifestyle we saw in the movies, and so I stayed out of the house a lot. At the time, I really enjoyed those activities.

In 1993, I remember violence starting that really surprised me. There was a Hutu leader who died on his way to the western province, and so the Hutus started killing the Tutsis because they claimed the Tutsis killed their leader. This was my first time seeing dead bodies. I saw a man and his wife and their dead bodies that were horribly killed in front of their house. It was hard to believe and hard to understand as a child. But after that, Tutsis started to flee from their homes and go to churches for protection. Tension rose in the country, and the Interahamwe started training in the roads, singing songs, and walking around with panga knives [machetes]. I couldn't understand what was going on.

Sometime near the end of 1993 and the beginning of 1994, my mom left us. She was someone who meant a lot to me. When we came home from school, we found everything clean and in place at home, but she was not there. We found a letter from her saying she had tried to be patient with the horrible life she had, and she tried to be patient with my dad and his alcoholism, but that she couldn't do it anymore. When I talk or think about this memory, it is so clear in my mind, and it feels like it just happened. She took my youngest brother with her, but left my sister, myself, and my younger brother. I still can't believe that she left us. That was the last day I saw my mom face to face.

Growing up, I was exposed to religion. My parents were Catholic, but we only went to church for big church holidays. I never saw them praying or living a Christian life. Between 1990 and 1994, there was a group of young men from the Pentecostal church who rented a house near ours. They would invite us to come to their church, but I wasn't interested. I just went there to eat food, but I wasn't interested in religion or God. Most of my memories of my life before the genocide were negative. It was not because we lacked things, but because my dad was a drunk.

The genocide started in 1994 when I was in primary three [third grade]. I have horrible memories from the genocide. On April 7, 1994, around 4:00 a.m., I heard a lot of gunshots...there were so many. It was my first time to hear gunshots like that, and I was in bed with my young[er] brother. He was so afraid and trembling, and I tried to pretend it was like something I had seen in the movies.

The gunshots continued that way until the morning, and when I woke up, I saw groups of men all around. They told me our former president's plane was shot down on its way from Tanzania. Although I was a child and didn't understand what was going to happen, when I saw the seriousness in the faces of the men, I knew something was wrong. I knew there was tension between the Tutsi and Hutu tribes, but I had no idea something like genocide could happen.

Although my dad told me to stay at home, he couldn't keep me there. After I washed my face and put on clothes, I left the house. When I got to the main road, I saw dead bodies and realized how serious things were. I saw men coming with property they had taken from others' houses, and I saw people killing one another. That was the first time I saw someone kill another person with my own eyes. Two men had an argument about the property they were taking from someone's house, and one took a gun and shot the other man. I was terrified, and immediately went back home. When I got home, my dad told me that the Hutus were furious because they thought the

Tutsis killed the Hutu president. I started discovering many things that I didn't know or understand before. I saw a lot of trenches dug in the ground. The Hutus said the Tutsis had dug the trenches because they were planning to kill Hutus and put their bodies in them. Then the Hutus said that now they would use the trenches for the bodies of dead Tutsis. I started to think about the things that happened before genocide, and I now understood why they asked about tribes, why we were separated by tribe, and why Tutsis were called bad names.

I wondered where my mom and young brother were, and how life would be for my dad, my sister, my brother, and I. It was difficult to see so many people in the community being killed and seeing their dead bodies. Someone I have never been able to forget was an old woman in the community. We used to go [to her house] often, and because she had many cows, she would give us milk. She was a good woman who was very respected in our community and it was so difficult to hear that she had been killed.

Since I was a child who spent most of my time outside of the house, it was very difficult for me to stay in the house, and so even during the genocide, I left the house often. A few months before the genocide started, we moved to a different part of Kigali, and not many people knew us in that community. I think this was one thing that really protected me during the genocide, because if we had stayed in our old community, everyone would have known that I was Tutsi. I thank God that the killers didn't know my family and me. I walked all around my community and heard about many people I knew who were killed. I saw a lot of dead bodies, and it was very difficult. I don't know why I kept walking around, but for some reason I didn't feel like I could stay at home.

I would sometimes follow the Interahamwe and Hutus and see them breaking into peoples' houses who were killed or who had run away. I wouldn't take anything, but I would follow them around. It was horrible to see the way that people were killed-even dogs don't die like that. They killed who they wanted and how they wanted. It's a difficult thing to remember. I still wonder what was going on inside of me as I walked around and saw all these horrible things. I don't know how to explain it.

Not all the Hutu people were bad. Some were good people and tried to help Tutsis. The Hutus could be outside and so they heard what was going on and would tell my dad. They suggested my dad and sister go outside with them, so that the Interahamwe would think they were Hutus as well. People in our community warned him that if he continued to stay in the house, the killers might start wondering why he wasn't going outside and become suspicious that he was a Tutsi. My dad tried to leave the house, and before he did, he sat down to read the Bible. This was the first time I had seen him reading the Bible, and I wondered what was going on. One day when my sister left the house, they said she had a Tutsi face, and they wanted to kill her. I thank God she didn't die.

The place where we lived in Kigali was in the middle of the fighting zone between the RPF and the Interahamwe. Most of the people who lived there left, but we stayed there with a few other families. There was a lot of shooting, and bombs were falling all around us. It was one of the first times I had to spend the whole day in the house, and I wondered what would happen to us. I thought, "I'm alive today, but tomorrow I will die." I had no hope or thought for the future, and I didn't think that the war would end. I thought things would continue the way they were. The next day, I pretended to go to the toilet, but I really went to see where other people had gone. I had a friend at that time who asked me why my family was still there, and he told me that there were rumors going around that all the people who stayed in that community were part of the RPF, and that the Interahamwe was going to come to kill everyone who stayed there. I went home and told my dad that tomorrow they were coming to kill us, and that he had to make a decision.

My dad took his identity card to see if he could change it. On the identity cards both tribes were written, and a line was used to cross off one of the tribes. My father was trying to erase the line that crossed off Hutu, and make a new line that crossed off Tutsi, so that if he was stopped, his identity card would read that he was a Hutu. Since I was a child, I didn't have an identity card, which is why I could move around. Sometimes people could identify people by the way they looked, but they couldn't do that with me. So we took a few things from our house, and moved to a refugee camp. After four hours there, my dad said he couldn't stay there and wanted to move us to another place where we used to live. He knew that we could be killed there because people knew us, but he wanted to go there anyway. While we were walking, my father had my sister, my brother, and I walk about one hundred meters in front of him. He told us to continue, no matter what happened to him, so that people wouldn't know that we were with him, and to continue to another refugee camp if anything happened to him. It was difficult though, because we would move about one hundred meters, and then stop to see what had happened to our father. During this time, I saw how horrible things were, far beyond what I had thought or was able to comprehend. I saw thousands and thousands of dead bodies on the side of the road, in the bush, and being eaten by dogs. The smell was awful. It was horrible. It's difficult for me to fully explain everything I saw and experienced. I can still see the images in my mind.

After walking for four hours, we reached the area of Kigali my father was taking us to. When we got there, people were surprised my dad was still alive, since everyone knew us there. We were unsure what would happen next. There was one lady who lived alone who welcomed us into her house. We started to hear that people wanted to kill us, and we heard that many of our relatives who lived in that area had already been killed. I thought that even though I was alive today, tomorrow I would be killed. We realized that if we stayed hiding in that place we would die of starvation.

At that time my dad started working as a tailor and asked my little brother and me to take his products to the markets in Kigali to sell them so that we could survive. The markets were only open for a few hours each day during the genocide, but people could still buy and sell. My brother and I went and managed to get some money, but we did not have many clients. We decided to start selling tobacco for cigarettes, and this was a good business. The Interahamwe took many things from the people they had killed, and so they had a lot of money to spend. These men often smoked and drank alcohol, so we sold a lot of tobacco to them and made money that way. I was eleven and my brother was nine. My sister had to stay in the house because she looked Tutsi. [Stereotypically, Tutsis are known for their lighter skin, height, and longer, narrower noses and faces. In contrast, Hutus are known to have darker skin, are shorter, and have wider noses and faces. These stereotypes were sometimes true, but did not apply to all Tutsis and Hutus. Due to the fact that the Tutsi-Hutu distinction was originally a class-based system that allowed for movement, and intermarriage, many peoples' appearances did not match their ethnicities.]

However, in May our business was not going well, and we needed to find some other business to do. A man we knew was making traditional beer mixed with drugs, which many men in the Interahamwe drank. He needed people to carry water for his beer, and he would pay anyone who was strong enough one hundred RWF for one jerry can of water from down in the valley. I couldn't carry a jerry can because I was too young, and my dad couldn't leave the house. However, my sister was older and stronger than I was, so she was able to carry jerry cans. The other girls in the community told my sister they would stay with her to protect her, and so my sister went with the girls to fetch water. She made about five hundred

RWF [less than one American dollar] each day by taking five jerry cans a day. One day however, they tried to kill her. The Hutu girls with her said she was their sister, but the killers questioned them asking how she could be their sister with her face and nose. They managed to rescue her, but it was very hard. From that time on, she had to stay inside.

It was about the middle of the genocide and bombs were dropped near where we lived. A fragment of a bomb killed my young[er] brother. Pieces of a bomb hit me and injured my right leg. From then on, I couldn't move on my own anymore, and I needed someone to carry me in and out of the house. After about two weeks, I used a stick to move short distances. I saw people being taken from the community, and I knew when they left they were going to be killed, and that they would not come back. People were killed and put in pits, but sometimes their bodies were left out and dogs would eat the bodies. People were killed in many terrible ways. The killers used panga knives [machetes], spears, swords, and wooden clubs, and people died terrible deaths. If you wanted to be killed by a gun, you had to pay the killers. Some rich families paid to be shot. Before the genocide stopped, my dad tried to leave the house, but he met someone who knew him. The man questioned my dad's identity card and claimed it had been changed. The man said he knew my dad's parents and that he knew he wasn't a Hutu. He told my dad he was a liar, and told him to go dig a pit for his body. If he refused, the man said he would kill him and leave his body out on the road. My dad was angry and refused to dig the pit. After a lot of arguing, the man let him go, saying others would kill him. From that day on my dad was afraid and didn't leave the house again.

Near the end of the genocide, we heard that the RPF was taking control of parts of the country. Although people had protected my dad, it was becoming very difficult for them to protect him because the fighting was increasing so much. So, every day he waited in our house to die. Our prayer was that the RPF would find us alive. One night, the RPF attacked our area, and the Interahamwe fled the place and took the Hutus in the area with them by force. My dad told them we were packing, as an excuse to stay, and in the morning, we found many people had left. That morning, many of the people I thought were dead came out of hiding. I was happy to see them, but it was also difficult to see them. They looked like living skeletons. The RPF came peacefully to ask us how we were doing, and to ask if we knew people that were alive. It was surprising to me, as we had always been told that the RPF had tails and big ears, and they had always been described like animals. So I was surprised to see they were peaceful people who were trying to help and not to hurt.

We were alive, but with no hope. Many places were destroyed, dead bodies were everywhere, and I wondered what would happen next. Even though we were alive today, I thought that we would die tomorrow. I felt like we were just living to die. Even many years after genocide, I felt this way about my life-that I was living to die.

The RPF took us to a high school in Kigali, where they kept us safe in a camp while the fighting was still going on in other parts of the country. This happened sometime near the end of June or early July [1994]. There were gardens where we got food, but we had to be careful because the Interahamwe had left landmines in the area before they left. On the sides of the road were dead bodies. It was so difficult to see the dogs eating the dead people that were lying around us. We stayed in that camp about a week, which was when they told us that we could return to our houses and that the RPF would keep us safe. However, many people were still doing what they wanted, and the country was not yet stable. At this time, I really wanted to know what had happened to my mother and my youngest brother who she had taken with her. I wondered if they were still alive or if they had died, but I had no idea. Some people told me that many of my relatives were dead. About a month after the genocide, I met my uncle who told me that my mom and brother were killed, but it was so hard for me to believe him. Even ten years after the genocide ended, I thought that I would still find my mother. It was so hard for me to believe that she was dead.

I can't remember everything, and it's hard for me to remember how everything happened. I saw many people being killed with my own eyes. I saw the Interahamwe take girls and kidnap them. I saw girls being raped and unbelievably horrible things done to their bodies. I saw people extremely wounded and killed in the most awful ways. I saw so much during the genocide since I was always outside walking around. I still don't know why I continued to walk around. It's hard for me to believe all these things, even though I lived through them. What I saw with my eyes I saw, but it's difficult to think about them and understand what really happened. When you're passing through hardship, you come to a point where your emotions are dead. When I think of where I am today, I wonder if I really was a human being during that time, because I had no emotions. It's so hard to comprehend all that I went through. I was walking like a dead person who was alive. I can't talk about my emotions or feelings during that time because there weren't any. I think I came to a point where my emotions no longer worked. I could see all these awful things, but I had no feelings.

What I saw became normal for me. I sometimes wondered why I was born into the broken family I had, and why I had to pass through all these things. I would ask, "Why me?" I wanted a good family, with enough food and clothing. But I came to the point where I thought my life was normal. I thought all I did just had to be part of life. As a child I didn't think deeply about all of this, I just thought about things on the surface. I didn't think about God at all, and so I never questioned him.

I'm at a good place now, because I can see the big picture and I'm better able to explain what happened. Honestly, eight years after the genocide I was trying to escape what happened, but I didn't realize that I was doing that. In my mind at the time, it was just how I lived life.

After the genocide, my dad, my sister and I lived together. During this time, I learned about the fate of my extended family. My dad was one of nine children before genocide, and only three survived [two died before the genocide]. All my grandparents were killed, and only two of my mom's brothers and sisters survived. Although I don't remember how many family members there were before genocide, I know it was a big family because each sibling of my parents had around six children. Although I don't know the exact number of people who were killed, I know there were many. I can count around five people from my mom's side who survived. I found out one of my aunties from my dad's side was still alive. Her husband and four of her six children were killed, but she survived with two children. She came to our home, and told my dad that girls needed to be raised differently than boys, and so she took my sister to raise her. After my auntie took my sister, two cousins were brought to live with us. One cousin left right away, and so I was left with my dad and the other cousin. My dad hadn't changed at all, and he started drinking more than he ever had before. He had a good job working for the Red Cross, but our life was the same because of his drinking. I was only twelve years old, but I started thinking about how I could survive on my own. During this time, I started drinking a lot of alcohol. I started school again, and although I was smart, eventually I failed out of school because of the choices I was making. When I was in primary five [fifth grade], I was walking by the side of the road and a car hit me, but I survived. People used to say that my life must have a purpose, because I first survived the bomb that killed my brother, and then I survived the car accident. When I got to primary six, I failed my national exam because I skipped school often and spent most of my time drinking and going to the cinema.

I didn't feel like school was important. With my group of friends, I started using marijuana and other drugs and drinking hard liquor. I did these things because that's what gave me comfort. I only lived for today, because I thought I would die tomorrow.

After failing my exam, I started a small business. I went into the markets in Kigali to sell plastic bags and carry things for people. I wanted to be on my own, eat what I wanted, use my money how I wanted, and not worry about my dad because he no longer took responsibility for our family. I decided to leave home because I no longer wanted to live with my father, and I did not have peace at home. I went into the heart of the city of Kigali, and I slept on the side of the road. I lived the life of a street kid, begging for money from *umuzungu* [white people], and trying to do small jobs. I saw many other kids stealing, but I didn't feel right about it. I stole something once, but I felt guilty about it.

I was around fourteen when I started living as a street kid. I met a man one day who asked me if I was a genocide survivor, and I told him I was. When he asked me if I had parents, I lied to him and told him I didn't. I'm not sure why I lied to him, but I did. He told me that I deserved a better life and shouldn't be living as a street kid, and he took me home with him. He gave me small jobs to do and allowed me to live with him at his home. He was a businessman, and I took care of his car and things without stealing. He was a Rwandan man who was living in exile in Burundi before the genocide. I lived with him for almost a year, and he took me back to school where I repeated primary six [sixth grade]. This time when I took the national exam, I passed it.

One day this man came to me and told me that he had found out that my dad was still alive. I still don't know how he got this information, but he was very compassionate to me. He thought my father was a Hutu, and thought that's why I had lied to him. However, because it was time for me to start secondary school, he said he would buy everything I needed for school and that we would deal with my father later. He wanted to meet my father, but told me that no matter what happened after he met my father, that I could still continue to live with him. At this time, I had not seen nor talked to my father or anyone in my family since I had left. No one knew what was going on in my life or where I was.

[Antoine initially agreed to attend secondary school. In Rwanda, secondary school consists of six years, which would be the equivalent of grades seven through twelve in the United States. Most Rwandan secondary schools are boarding schools, although some will take day scholars as well. Antoine's schooling was interrupted first by the genocide, and again by poverty, so he was not the typical age of a seventh-grader in the United States. Antoine was part of a generation of Rwandan children whose access to education was greatly impacted by the genocide, and the poverty it created for child survivors.]

After about two weeks of staying at the boarding school, I decided I didn't want to live there any longer. The school was in the village, and life was not easy there. So I took everything he bought for me and sold some things, gave some to friends, and I went back to the streets. Being back in the city was difficult because I was trying to hide myself from the man who had sent me to school. He was in the city for business often and I didn't want him to see me. One day, however, he saw me, and I ran away from him. He told some other street children to tell me not to worry, that he wasn't angry and that he just wanted to talk to me. I was about seventeen years old; I was using drugs often. The small business I was trying to do was failing and a lot of my money was going towards drugs. I was also gambling, and sometimes the older street kids would take the little money I had from me.

This is the point in my life where I hit rock bottom. Things were at their worst. It was hard to buy soap, clothes, and shoes. I had long hair and had lice in my hair and on my body. I would go two weeks without washing myself. When I got money, I would buy food, drugs, and alcohol, and then I would sleep on the side of the road.

My aunt was in Kigali in a taxi when she saw me on the streets. She pulled the taxi over, got out, and pulled my ear. When I turned around and saw it was her, I was speechless. She was about to cry and asked me why I was here. I felt like it was a stupid question because I was so angry with her. She had taken my sister and left me living with my dad, even though she knew that he was a drunk and that he beat me. I was carrying so much anger, but my emotions were broken. Nobody cared about me. It was my life, and I wondered what she was doing here. She saw that I was shocked, and so she asked me if I would come with her. I agreed to come, and she took me to her home. It was 2000 when I went to live with her, and it had been six years since I had seen or talked to my sister, but I didn't want to see my dad. Even before genocide, my family was broken because of my dad's drinking, and the few years I had lived with him after the genocide, it was the same. I didn't care about him, and I didn't think about him or when I would see him. I had enough of him.

My aunt took me home, gave me clothes, gave me a shower, and cut my hair. I honestly don't know what was going on with my mind and my emotions. I didn't think about anything; I just adapted to my environment, whatever it was. So when I changed environments, my life changed as well. Now I had a place to sleep, I had food, and it was much better. However, my emotions were still the same: I wasn't sensitive to anything, and I didn't care about anything. I felt like I was living to die. If not tomorrow, then maybe the next day. I was waiting for death to come.

My aunt started asking me lots of questions, but I wouldn't answer them. She gave me many rules for staying in the compound. When I think back, I see how God protected me while I was living there. I did break the rules, but always in secret so my aunt didn't find out what I was doing. One day my aunt sent me to visit my sister at school. It had been six years since I had seen her, and I wondered what it would be like. My aunt packed food for me to bring her, packed some gifts for her, gave me money, and showed me which bus to take and how to get to her boarding school. I don't remember anything I was feeling. When I got to school I asked for her, and some nice girl took me over to the dormitory where she stayed. When my sister came out and saw me, she cried and ran away from me. I was shocked by her emotions because I didn't have any. I was annoyed with her because I had come all the way to see her, and I now wanted to go back. I wondered what she was doing. The girls went to get her and brought her back outside with me. We sat together for about an hour, although now I don't remember what our conversation was about. My emotions were totally dead.

After that, my aunt asked me to go back to school, and I agreed to try. When I got to school, I continued to use drugs, but my aunt didn't know. Even when I lived at home, I used drugs there, but no one knew because I didn't leave home. I used marijuana the most, but it was my secret. I used drugs heavily for about four years. Sometimes my aunt left me in the shop, and I would steal small amounts of money to buy marijuana. When I was at school, I had more freedom than I had at home, and in my secondary school, many people used drugs. There was no one to control me, and so I would leave school to use. However, I still did well and I was first in my class at school. Because of this, when I went home everyone thought that I was doing well and that I had changed. However, the reality was that I was empty inside. I felt like it would be better to die than to live. When people came together to dance, sing, and talk, I would always leave. I used the radio as a way to get away from people. I didn't have the heart to feel, or the ability to receive people. Those days I still thought I would meet my mom somewhere. She meant so much to me and nothing will replace her love for me. I wasn't a good child and my mom was troubled by my bad behavior. I still felt guilty for how I acted because she was the person who loved me more than anyone.

It was really hard at that time because I didn't realize how broken I was. I thank my aunt because she gave me everything I needed; she tried to listen to me, and she was patient with my brokenness and my bad behavior. I now started to ask myself deep questions. I asked, Why? Why is life like this? Was I really born to live like this? I decided that it was better for me to die. I wasn't able to commit suicide, but I wished I would die. My life had no meaning. Even though I was doing well in school, I just did it. Some days I wanted to drop out of school, some days I wanted to join the army, and I was often wondering why life was like this. I was around eighteen at this time, and I was in senior one and senior two [seventh and eighth grade] when I started to think about all these things. I felt empty and I felt like it was enough. There is no meaning to life. There is no reason to live.

At this point, I became more interested in God. As I mentioned, before genocide, there was a group of Pentecostal men that lived near my home. Although I wasn't interested in God as a child, and I just went there to eat food, I remembered their teachings. They talked about a God who created everything, who was able to do anything, and they talked about Jesus. I started to pray, and asked God, "Is this how you created me to live?" I told Him that if He wanted my life to continue in this way, that I would prefer to die. But if what the men had said was true, then I asked God to change my life because it was so hard to bear. I joined the Protestant groups in my high school, and when they preached, I felt guilty. I would stand up for prayer, but after I left church, I would continue my lifestyle of using drugs and drinking. I began to feel afraid and felt like I shouldn't play with God by going to church and saying I would live my life for God, but then never changing. I decided that I wouldn't go to church anymore because I wasn't changing my lifestyle. The feelings I had then are so hard to explain.

I started to face reality when I gave my life to Christ. When I was nineteen, I was in senior two [eighth grade], and there was a time when the electricity was cut off for almost one week. This was a big problem for me because of my habits. During the day I would go to class, and after class I would sneak out and go in the village to get drugs. When I snuck back into the boarding school, all I wanted was to eat and sleep. Then around 2:00 a.m., I would wake up to study. This is how I continued to perform well in school, even though I was using drugs. The week the electricity was out was the week before our final exams, and I was worried I would go back to my aunt with bad results and that she would start wondering what I was doing. I started praying, and asking God again why my life was the way it was. I asked God to bring back the electricity, and I asked Him to change my life. I told God that if He changed me, then I would live the rest of my life for Him. One night I snuck out with six [of] my friends into the city to get drugs. I was using so much at that time that I felt like I would go crazy if I didn't get drugs.

On the way back to school, we met someone coming from our school who told us the electricity was back on. When he said that, my heart started pounding, as I remembered my prayer. As we continued to walk back to school, I started crying, but because it was dark outside, no one noticed. My friends wondered why I was so quiet, but they thought it was because I had taken too many drugs. As I was crying, I was begging God for answers. Why is my life like this? Why am I like this? Did You really create me and intend for me to live this horrible life? Why? Why? Why? I cried the whole way home. I asked God again if He could change my life. I asked because I felt like it was impossible for Him to change me. I promised Him, "If You change my life, then I will give You the rest of my life, and I will serve You."

When we got back to school, I tried to dry my tears. It was Friday, which was the day when students would gather to pray. I gave my things to my friends to take back to my room, and told them I would find them there later. They asked me where I was going, and when I told them I was going to pray, they thought that I was going crazy. I told them to stop asking me questions, that I was fine, and to take my things and the drugs I had just bought back to my room. When I went to pray, I don't remember anything that was going on. All I remember is that they read a verse from Job 38, but I don't remember the [specific] verse [from that chapter]. When they read the verse and were preaching, I was crying and shaking the whole time. I don't remember anything the preacher said. The only thing I remember is when they asked if anyone wanted to give their life to Christ. I stood up and said *yes*, and they prayed for me, although now I don't remember anything that they said in their prayers. I went back to my seat still shaking and crying. My whole body was shaking like someone who had a fever. After the gathering finished, others entered the room to watch the news, but I kept sitting there. After about thirty minutes, I realized there were other people around me, and I realized they might wonder what I was doing. So I lifted up my head to try to watch TV, but I was just waiting for the news to finish so I could leave. I skipped dinner that night and went into my room so I could be alone while they ate. This was when I cried a lot. Something was going on inside me. I was crying and shaking so violently that my whole bed was shaking, and I felt like something was leaving me. There were different sounds coming out of my mouth, and I felt like fear and spirits were being lifted from me. After that I had peace and finally slept.

I woke up in the morning, and I was a new person. Before, we used to sneak out of school before class started to use drugs, and so that morning my friends came to get me to go with them as usual. But that morning I refused to go with them. My friends didn't understand what was going on. I didn't say anything that whole day in class. The next day I went to the Protestant student gathering to pray, and when my friends saw me going, they thought that I was crazy. Honestly, I didn't realize what was going on. I went again to pray on Friday, and they prayed for me again. This was the time I decided that I wanted to follow God and that I wanted to be a Christian. This is when I started that journey.

However, I still didn't want to deal with my emotions. I enjoyed my new life and I was committed to following God at any cost, but I still didn't want to go deep within myself to deal with my emotions. However, I was committed to God, and began fasting, praying, and reading the Bible. People started seeing this and saw that I had the ability to preach and share God's word. I was invited to be included in different ministries in the school, and my relationship with God grew through that. Since God had delivered me from such an awful life, I wanted to be as holy as possible, and so I spent a lot of time in prayer and fasting. Others saw me as an example, but there were so many things I didn't understand. I asked God why he had allowed all these things to happen to me. I started missing my mom so much. For the first time, I started thinking about my emotions, and they started to come alive again. Since I didn't have any answers for my questions, I chose to live with that and continue to follow God. In order to escape my questions and emotions, I spent a lot of time in prayer and fasting. In one way, this time seeking God played a big role in my life, but in another way, this was just a way to escape my problems. I chose to be alone, and I didn't like to speak to people.

Honestly, I was angry and I was broken, but since I knew a good God, I tried to spend all my time with Him. I gained more knowledge from the Bible and from prayer, but there were still things that were hard for me to understand. From this time, I learned that despite the fear to face reality, despite ignorance, despite lack of understanding, if you come to God, He will change things in your life. When you spend time with God and lean on Him with everything you have, He will do big work in your life.

After I finished senior six [twelfth grade], I continued with two and a half years of university. While I was in university, I helped lead the Christian group at my school. Although I was going deeper with God, there was still something like a box in my heart that I didn't want to open. People saw me as a good guy who was working hard, but it was hard for me to connect with other people. It was easy for others to come to me, and I could help them. They told me they appreciated me and that I had helped them. Honestly, even though God used me, it was only by His grace because I was still so broken then. It's hard for me to understand how God used me when I was in that state. That's why it's always been about Him and not about me. The truth was I didn't want to face the reality of what had happened to me. When people tried to talk about the genocide, I would tell them I was okay because I didn't want to talk about the things that touched me that deeply. I escaped these emotions by ignoring them and not talking about them; I would only discuss things on the surface.

Many people still identified by tribes and divided themselves by Hutu and Tutsi, but God was working in my life because I felt comfortable associating with and talking to anyone, regardless of their tribe. I was able to share with everyone, and looking back I'm able to see how God's hand was at work, even though I didn't realize it at the time. However, there were still other areas of my life that I hadn't allowed God to work in yet.

When I was twenty-seven years old, I had the opportunity to work with an organization called Youth with a Mission (YWAM), where they helped me face my emotions to deal with them and not ignore them. I did a program with YWAM called Discipleship Training Program [DTS], where we started to study the nature and character of God. I began to question God in deep ways. I questioned how the God I was studying and learning about could have allowed these things to happen to me. I asked God many difficult questions. I realized that God had been already working in me to heal me, even though I didn't realize it at the time. I thought that the time I spent in prayer and fasting was just a part of being righteous and holy, but it was also a part of my healing and what helped restore me.

When I look back at what I was preaching during secondary school, I see how it was full of my brokenness. Despite that, many people came to Christ through my preaching. People trusted me and came to me for counseling and for the word of God, and I was able to help them, even though I couldn't help myself. The real change came when I started DTS with YWAM.

My sister had gotten such healing through her time in DTS that she supported me to do the program after she was finished. She told me that before I could go ahead and continue with life, I needed to first be healed. No one else wanted me to do DTS because they saw I had a university degree and thought it was time for me to get a job and get on with my life. People saw me on the outside, and thought I was fine, but they didn't know how I was still broken on the inside. When people asked me why I was doing the program and what my purpose was in life, it was a hard question for me to answer. I thought about being a pastor, and I wanted to preach the gospel because I saw the power it had to change someone's life. I knew this was something I could give to people. I wanted to reach people to give them the good news of Christ.

When I came to DTS I couldn't focus on my studies because I was so broken. When we started talking about the nature and character of God, I broke out crying because I saw how hardened I was to listening to God. I was confused—how could this righteous and holy God allow these things to happen to me? I questioned God with all the things I went through in my life, from the broken family I was born into, to the horrible things that happened in the genocide in Rwanda. So who was this righteous God, this holy God, this just God? It was a hard week of studying and questioning. It was hard to understand because my heart was so hard, but despite that, I learned the truth. After the week of studying the nature and character of God, we studied God as a father. This was another hard concept for me to understand. It made me think of my biological father—how could God be a father? It was hard, although it brought me a lot of healing.

To be honest, even thinking about God as a father today is hard for me because it brings up many wounds I have from my biological father that are not yet fully healed. My biological father is still alive, and I occasionally talk to him. He has a phone now so I can call him. After the genocide, he started a new family and has a wife and four other children. He still drinks and lives the same lifestyle. I pray that God will change his life. I had one deep conversation with him two years ago [in 2012], and I sensed that he knew he needed to change his life. However, he's still facing hardship and hasn't made changes. I don't really know what's going on inside of him and what he thinks about his life and the choices he's made, but I get the feeling that he doesn't want to end life the way he's been living it.

So through DTS, I had the chance to face myself, my brokenness, and ask God the many questions that I had. It's opened the door to me, and now when I come before God, I bring everything to him. I now express my emotions and feelings to God and try to keep facing the reality of life, even when it is difficult. I've had a chance to go through the healing process in different ways, and I really enjoy my relationship with God and relationships with people. There are so many changes to how I interact with people now. People now see me as a good guy, even though I was not always like that. I thank God that He's helped me learn how to live with people and build healthy relationships despite my past. Now things are getting better. I'm growing in my faith, and I know my life has purpose and that I'm here for something big. I'm looking forward to what God created me for. I know there is a lot to do, and I've already seen God do so much in my life. He's taken me through different steps of healing, and I've seen good things become of it. I'm curious about what the future will hold because I know there is still a lot to come and a lot more that will happen in my life.

The first eight years after genocide, I lived in brokenness and had no hope. I felt it was better to die than to live. The next eight years I was living as a Christian and experienced some changes in my life, but I was still afraid to face reality because it was hard. I tried to cover up the reality with my relationship with God. I felt like I was getting somewhere, and that although life was not good on Earth, it would be in heaven, so I had hope for that. I used the hope of heaven to ignore what had happened in my life, and I focused on the future life with God in heaven rather than what was happening in my life on earth. The past four years is when God brought me to the light. I allowed his light to shine on my brokenness and take me through the process of healing. It's not yet finished, and I look forward to the rest of my life because I still have a lot of life to live. Now, I don't only have hope in heaven, but I also have hope for what God created me for on earth.

In short, it's hard to think about God when we try to think about Him in our human way. One thing I would like to teach others is to see God for who He really is and not see Him based upon our lives and situations. We need to learn to see things the way God sees them. This is hard because it means we need to face the realities of our lives, and this is a challenge for many people. We don't want to go inside ourselves and face what is there. It's easier to pretend and live like life is good. Many people use drugs and sex as ways to avoid the brokenness we have in our hearts and the reality of our lives. In our brokenness, we have so many questions. Does God exist? Is He really God? How can He be who He says He is? Even though we ask those questions, the reality is we don't want to seek out the answers because it forces us to go deeply into our hearts and our pain, which is a difficult place to go.

For some people, they are in the middle of going through difficult times, and so it's very hard to face your past when the present is also challenging. However, God is a good God, and when we come to Him he will help us understand things. Sometimes we go to people, but people can't fully explain what and why things happen in our lives. When we choose to really come to God, He helps us and gives us understanding about what's going on. We will find healing because God doesn't just cover the wound and tell you it's okay, He takes us through the process of healing. Once this process and healing happens, then we will start living life with the freedom and fullness God intends for us. It's a hard process, but we need to face reality one step at a time. Don't judge God by situations, but allow God to judge situations. When we expose everything to the light, the outcome will be good, and we will have freedom. As Christians, we can't live like Christ in our brokenness, because we can't present Him to others in that way. So if we really want to understand Christ, understand his love, grace, mercy, and character, so that we can present him to others, we need to first come to Christ and allow him to change us. Let us face the reality, whatever it may be. We all face brokenness in different ways.

Many people have challenges in their families; some are facing divorce, others are struggling with addiction. There are a lot of things going on around the world, and it's hard to understand God when we try to judge Him by these situations. Often we pray, but our prayers don't get anywhere. We don't live a life of freedom because we can't get there until we face ourselves and allow God to heal us. Let's be bold enough to face who we are. This will show us what we need to change, and what to hold on to. Don't worry if you feel like it's too hard—God can change everything for those who believe in

Him and allow Him to work in their life. My life is a testimony for that. I am amazed at where I'm at and question if it's me or someone else. Know that God created you and knows where to touch your life in order to restore your life and bring you back into his original plan for you. Let's be bold enough to face what we are going though and allow God to judge our situations.

CHAPTER 2:
CLEMENT & ELYSE

Region: Gitarama

Located in the southern province of Rwanda, Gitarama is known for cassava plants that are prepared traditionally in the form of a delicious dish, called *ubugali*: cassava flour combined with water that is cooked until it becomes a doughy consistency that can be ripped apart and dipped in sauces. It is a dish unique to Rwanda and sharing *ubugali* is a cultural tradition.

During the genocide, the most notable place in Gitarama was the Catholic Church Kabgayi, where many Tutsis in the area fled for safety. Tragically, this church was transformed into a death camp, as refugees waited in horrific living conditions for Interahamwe militia who came daily to select people to kill. Local clergymen were also involved in the killings. Gacaca court—informal court where perpetrators of the genocide addressed survivors—judges have reported an estimated sixty-four thousand Tutsi men, women, and children were killed in Kabgayi.[3]

<hr />

[3] https://www.newtimes.co.rw/section/read/7114

The following two men are from Gitarama. Clement and Elyse are cousins who grew up together. Clement lived with his parents and siblings in one house, while Elyse lived next door in their grandmother's house along with his mother and baby brother. Only months apart in age, as children these cousins were often mistaken as twins, and spent much of their lives together. During the genocide, they were separated. Elyse ended up in Kabgayi with his mother, brother, and Clement's father. Clement was in hiding in various areas with his mother and siblings. Their stories reference one another and the family members they have in common.

Both Clement and Elyse live in Kigali now and remain close friends. They can often be found watching a soccer game, laughing, and joking with one another. Elyse is a Good News International community member who went through a sponsorship program to complete his bachelor's degree. Clement is a staff member of Good News International and provided all translating services for this book.

IV: Clement Ndayisaba

Name: Clement Ndayisaba
Year and place of birth: 1986, Gitarama, Ruhango District, South Province
Age during the genocide: seven to eight
Family members killed during genocide: four aunts and other extended family members
Family members who survived genocide: mother and father, three aunts, cousins, two sisters
Schooling completed: master's degree
Occupation: IT for Good News Guesthouse and sponsorship coordinator for Good News International
Currently living with: wife and child
Language spoken for interview: English [Clement was the interpreter for all the interviews that were conducted in Kinyarwanda].

Hopping off the motos, we pay the drivers; they spin, engines revving, and disappear into the distance, leaving puffs of exhaust in their wake. We turn and begin to make our way up a steep hill, as cobblestones turn to dirt, and small clouds of dust lift off the ground and settle again. The road bends and winds. Laughing, we reminisce about the events of the day. Our easy English and contrasting looks draw curious stares.

I remember many things from when I was young. We were a middle-class family, and we had everything we needed. We had four cows, and our house was near my grandmother's house, who was living with my auntie and my cousin. Our aunts lived in Kigali, and we often went to visit them. Our family was very close. We had many friends in the area and had good relationships with the people around us.

Things first started changing in 1992. There were two places we went to fetch water, and I often went with my cousin. We went with other children our age to bring water for our families, and we often joked and played with them. One day in 1992, our friends started calling us names, like snakes. We didn't understand why they were calling us snakes, but they called us that all the time. At first, we thought they were just joking, but later it became more serious. One day, we went to fetch water early in the morning, but they wouldn't let us get water. We kept being pushed to the back of the line, while those who had arrived after us were getting water before us, until everyone was finished getting water. We asked our parents why we were being treated this way, and although they knew the reason, they never explained what was going on. It continued to get more difficult for my cousin and me to get water, and so we started to go to a different place to fetch water. Although it was far from home, we had no choice.

One day I was going alone to get water, and I met a man who was around eighteen years old. He took my jerry cans from me and didn't allow me to get any water. He kept my jerry cans and wouldn't let me go back home. After two hours, he took rope and tied my arms behind my back and made me sit on the ground. I was sitting there and couldn't move because my arms were tied.

Many people passed by me to get water, but no one asked what he was doing to me or why such a small child was tied on the ground. No one cared about me, although many of the people who passed by knew me. Around 11:00 a.m., my mother came looking for me because I had left early in the morning to get water and had not returned for a long time. When the man saw my mother coming, he pushed me down into the ground and ran away. My mother came, untied me, got our jerry cans, and we went back home. We couldn't tell anyone what had happened because our parents were also being abused. This is how I noticed things changing in Rwanda, and how our relationships with our friends and neighbors changed.

In 1993 tensions rose, and it became more serious. At that time, we learned that we were Tutsis and the other people were Hutus and that Tutsis were bad people and unwanted in our society. There was fear everywhere. When I was in primary two [second grade], teachers would have Tutsis stand up and sit on one side of the room, and Hutus stand up and sit on the other side of the room. If we didn't know what ethnicity we were, teachers told us to go home and ask our parents what we were. This is how many children found out whether they were Hutu or Tutsi.

In 1993, it became more dangerous because of the political instability in the country. The political parties were fighting, and we could feel that things were different. There were many different political parties, but because most of them were not happy with the country leadership, the political parties in power started mobilizing local people by giving them flags, uniforms, and weapons. I remember there was a man who was a friend of my parents living near us. Two months before the genocide started, he came with a gun to take my dad. He took him somewhere for one week, but we didn't know where he went. They beat and abused him in many different ways because they knew he was Tutsi. After this man had taken my father, he came to our house and pretended like he was a pastor starting a new church. Many people were involved in the church, and many local people from the area joined. He started teaching people new songs, but the songs were all about killing. The songs were about killing the demons, and many people, including my cousin and I, went to the church to sing with them. During the genocide, we discovered that the songs were really about killing Tutsis. When the people came to attack our families, they were singing these same songs. We realized these songs were not about the devil, but he was training people to sing songs they would later sing as they killed during the genocide.

On April 6 [1994], I was tending the cows, and that night the president's plane was shot down. In the morning, there was a big train of cars of white people who were all driving with their country's flags. When I asked, I learned they were ambassadors, leaders of non-governmental organizations (NGOs), and other important people who were all going back to their countries. I was told they were not allowed to take any Rwandans from the country.

Our parents knew what had happened in 1959 and 1961 [ethnic violence broke out between Hutus and Tutsis, resulting in thousands of Tutsi deaths], and so they knew there were going to be killings, but since we were just children, it felt like a movie. We were excited to see all the activity, and we were not mature enough to realize we were in danger.

The next evening, our parents and Tutsi neighbors organized themselves because they knew our houses would be burned, our cows would be eaten, and we would be killed. They planned for the children and wives to stay in the houses, and for the men to circle the houses to protect us. Many of our Hutu neighbors were very involved in the killings and were motivated to attack us. At six thirty in the evening, people came and started burning the fence surrounding our house. The men put out the fire, and those who burned the fence left. We did not sleep at all that night because we were so afraid. The next day, things became more dangerous. That day the killers came with guns, machetes, spears, knives, and other weapons. All the killers were people we knew because they were our neighbors. There was a military camp nearby, and so they were equipped with some militia. They came that day, and they attacked. I remember that they threw a grenade on the roof of our house, and after they threw that grenade, we had no choice, we immediately left. Everyone was running, and it was chaos because we were all running on our own. My mother took myself and my two sisters, and we escaped to another family's home nearby, and we stayed there in hiding.

When the genocide started, the killers were looking for men. They wanted to kill my father and myself, and at that time they were not as focused on killing my mother and sisters. They came and took everything from our house. They killed our four cows and ate the meat from the cows. They took everything from the house of my grandma as well. They took everything we had. Then they started destroying our houses. It was totally destroyed down to the foundation.

My father left with my cousin, aunties, and grandma. My mom, sisters, and I went a different way. At first, my mother's family was not targeted to be killed, and so we went there. Unlike the Hutu people who lived near my home, the Hutu people in the area that mother's family is from were kind and helped keep us safe. We stayed there in hiding, and my father joined us there. However, as time passed my mother's family also became targeted, and after two days of hiding there it became dangerous as more Hutu people were pressured to begin killing. When we left my mother's family, I was with my mom, my two sisters, and my father. We didn't know where my grandma, aunties, and cousins were. Since they were looking for my dad and me, my dad left us to keep us safe. I was too young to go with my father, and so I stayed with my mom and sisters who were four years old and nine months old. We went to people we didn't know and stayed with them. Because the killers were searching for me, I was hidden under the bed in their house, while my mom and my sisters were able to be in the house in the open. One day, the killers came into the house to search for people in hiding. They came into the house with big sticks and were searching under the beds with the big sticks to see if anyone was there. I was hiding there, and I was so fortunate that they didn't find me. We stayed there longer, and during the nights, we were taken into the banana and sorghum bushes. We stayed in the bushes for about one week before we were taken to another family because things had become too dangerous for us there.

While we were in hiding there, my father had moved to a Catholic school called Kabgayi, where he found my aunties, grandma, and cousins. We didn't know how they had gotten there, but they stayed there for the rest of the genocide. Killers came to that compound and killed people every day. They came in the morning to kill and came back every morning. Many Tutsis from all over the country had come to Kabgayi to live and seek protection, but they were being killed day by day. The killers came each morning in big buses and took people away to kill them. They started with the men. They took my dad three times, but he managed to escape every time. When they would take people from Kabgayi to enter the buses, my father would circle the bus and then hide in the bush. Then he would return to the compound. He did this three times. Some people in Kabgayi died of hunger, disease, and dirty water. It was a horrible life and many people died there.

The RPF arrived June 2 to liberate the area we were in. They took us to Ruhango because the RPF had already stopped the genocide there. On the way to Ruhango we passed by our homes. Our banana trees had been cut down, and our homes destroyed. We couldn't even recognize that that's where our homes had been. We lived for a few weeks in Ruhango, and then we had to return to our home area at the beginning of July. When we returned, all our neighbors had left with the killers and fled to the Democratic Republic of the Congo [formerly Zaire]. There was no one there, and since we didn't have a house, we lived in the houses of our neighbors who had fled. Some of them were killers, but some of them were not. We stayed there with other Tutsis who survived from our area.

After about one month, those who hadn't [been] killed, started to come back once they heard that it was safe. My father decided that we shouldn't continue to live in other people's houses, and so my father cut down trees to make our own house—if I can call it a house—back where the old one stood. Many people started coming back to the area. I would estimate that about sixty percent of the Tutsis who lived in my area were killed.

As a child, I was traumatized during the genocide. We were living a horrible life, and it's hard to fully explain what I was thinking and feeling. I remember staying in banana bushes all night long in the rain, hiding from the killers, and not knowing where my family members were, or if I would survive until the morning. We didn't know what would happen or where we would go next.

Some schools started back in September, although there were no teachers and few students. However, it was a symbol that life had started again. Our parents sent us to school to try to create stability. Although we would be safe one day, we woke up the next not knowing if the killing was going to start again. We didn't know if life was going to continue. However, we started to see changes. The Red Cross came to give things like jerry cans, food, and clothing to families. Other NGOs started to help people, and the government started to reorganize people.

We were able to see things were becoming more secure, but we were still traumatized and only able to live life one day at a time. We were not able to care about these changes. Teachers came back, even though many were not qualified. My father started to reorganize our family. He started making bricks to try to make our house, and after some time another NGO came to help rebuild houses that were destroyed. Life continued this way after the genocide, and the society was rebuilding. However, there was still distrust among people, as we didn't know who had been involved in the killings and who had not. Some people who had killed were ashamed, and they were afraid of revenge killings. In this manner, there was still distrust from both Hutus and Tutsis. According to what we knew, those who had killed had not returned to the area. The government had started finding the killers and putting them in prison. All this happened in 1994.

In 1995 things had stabilized more, and we went back to an organized school. The government continued to find those who participated in killings to put them in prison. Relationships were getting better between people, but of course there was still mistrust. Even our parents had been traumatized. We had everything, and now we were living with nothing. We only had one set of clothes that we wore, yet we saw other children running around wearing the clothes we had before genocide. There was one child wearing our good pants and shorts, and we wanted to fight with him because we had nothing. His father wore our father's suit.

Some people were kind and started bringing back what they took. Some neighbors brought back the doors and the windows they had taken from our house. It showed us that some people were caring and able to help. This is how life continued, but it was very difficult for us. Finding food was a struggle, and so it was hard for me to study or to put effort into my schooling. Things were bad. The first time I got my school report, I was the tenth to last student in the class. I wasn't encouraged to study, and my parents only sent me to school because they had to, but there was no purpose for them to send me.

Two years after the genocide, we realized life was going to continue, and that continuing life was our only choice. My parents started working hard, cultivating for food, and buying new cows. We were encouraged to work and to study, and we saw the government was stable and that things were improving in Rwanda. That's when I realized that I needed to continue school and that I needed to put effort into my studies. I finished primary school, and we were still living with my cousin. However, since my cousin lost his mother during the genocide, he went to live with our aunt in Kigali. We both passed primary school and went to secondary school, and my cousin and I visited each other often.

In senior one [seventh grade] I started to think about my life and plan for my future. After senior three [ninth grade], I passed the national exam and continued to senior four [tenth grade]. I knew the struggle of my past life, and I saw my studies as a way to improve my life and my situation. I saw it as a way to escape the difficult life I had been living. This encouraged me to do as much as I could to go from one level to another. When I went home during the holidays and saw the quality of life of people there, I was motivated to keep working hard in school so that I wouldn't have to return there to live in those conditions. In senior five [eleventh grade], I realized that God was shaping me for a better life. After senior six [twelfth grade], I passed my national exams and received a scholarship to go to university. During university is when things changed a lot for me, because that's when I started making friends and seeing that life in Rwanda was changing. I continued to see big changes in my life and envision big things for my future. I saw the better future I was in the process of shaping. I was encouraged to continue striving for that.

Right now I'm completing my master's and have some wonderful friends. I really had hope for the future when I started university. The progress that was being made in my family and within my own life gave me hope. In the past, I would've never thought that I could have gone to university. The achievements and progress allowed me to see that despite the horrors of the past, good things were still possible. I met with other people and we shared our testimonies of the past, and how God has taken us from one level to another level. God has showed me the better future that He has for me. The past is the past, and we can't change it, but we have power over our future. We can't do anything about our past, but the future is in our hands. This encouragement has kept me moving forward. I have focused on and used my energy on my studies, especially in university. God still gives me hope for the future for myself, for my family, and for things that I don't even know about yet.

We have achieved what we never could've dreamed of before. This helps encourage us to move forward and to not stray away from the plans God has for us. If you were to see me now, you would not believe I was the same person I told you about in 1994.

I have many lessons I want to teach people. One of them comes from the Bible. Jesus gives us a new law in the New Testament—to love people. I want to remind people to love one another and to respect one another as human beings. When you respect people, you see them as opportunities, rather than as problems. See your friends, colleagues, and neighbors as opportunities, not as problems. Do not be tempted into hate and anger.

Also, I want people to know that God is able to do anything. In Rwanda, we are people who have been through many horrors and challenges, and the way we have seen God restore our lives is so special. God can restore everyone's life in this way. He can create new life, and He is not limited. He can do all things.

The third lesson is to let people know that the future is a self-decision. Whenever you make a decision in your life, there is no reason not to achieve what you plan. Let God guide you and listen to his guidance. If what you plan is good and in God's will, and if you work for it, you will achieve it.

V: Elyse Iradukunda

Name: Elyse Iradukunda
Year and place of birth: 1986, Gatenga, Kigali
Age during genocide: seven
Family members killed during genocide: mother and brother, approximately twelve extended family members
Family members who survived genocide: ten extended family members
Schooling completed: bachelor's degree in finance
Occupation: manager of microfinance in Amasezerano Bank in Kigali
Currently living with: his wife Scholastique and two children
Language spoken for interview: Kinyarwanda and English; portions spoken in Kinyarwanda interpreted into English by Clement Ndayisaba

We continue, in and out of Kinyarwanda and English, questioning in one language and replying in the other. Clement interprets when needed. Pausing, eyes closing, his mind recounts images it has not ever willingly conjured from the recesses of his memory. The fresh air, green branches, and walls of the garden provide a safe reminder of the reality of the present and its distance from the perilous past. Hours pass as the conversation continues.

Before genocide we lived in Gitarama. We were still young, and so we saw things happen, but didn't understand that it was related to ethnic groups. Eventually, we started to understand why people were being treated differently. Before the genocide I lived with my mom, my young[er] brother, and my grandmother. My father died before the genocide when I was a baby, so I never knew him. I was the firstborn, and my younger brother was about four years younger than I was. We had everything we needed, such as clothes, cows, and other belongings that classified us as a good family. We were all Catholic and went to church every Sunday, but because we were young, we didn't think much about God, and we just went to church out of routine. I had many joyful times with family and friends before the genocide. I had a good life and good relationships, and I really enjoyed my life.

Relationships with people in my community were good, although things started to change during the time leading up to the genocide. When we would go to get water, we realized that we were being treated differently than we had been before. We were discriminated against and called different names, and even children were told if they were Hutu or Tutsi. In schools, there were divisions in classrooms, where the teachers would tell the Tutsis to go on one side of the room and the Hutus to go on the other side. Even with our neighbors there were divisions and we were not treated the same as the others. Our community was about ninety-eight percent Hutu, and about two percent Tutsi and Twa. When I first learned my ethnicity, I did not take it seriously, but when the genocide started and they started killing us, destroying our property, and taking our houses, I realized how dangerous it was and that we were targeted.

The day the genocide started, things totally changed. The first day of the genocide, our neighbors came and killed our cows, destroyed our houses, and cut down our banana trees. We immediately ran away from our homes and hid ourselves in the bushes and forests. We were first hidden by the Hutu people who were our other neighbors. They were not involved in the killings, and since they had a good relationship with our grandparents, they couldn't let us be killed. We stayed with them for a week or two. They protected us, fed us, and gave us everything we needed. However, the killers found out that they were hiding Tutsis, and we were all going to be killed if we stayed. They took us to a place where they knew other Tutsis were hiding. After that, someone from that family took us away during the night. He walked with us to the camp where the refugees were. We had to go at night, because during the day there were so many killers all around. There were five of us together at that time. I was with my mother, my brother, a neighbor, and another person from my extended family. We continued moving and hiding until we got to the Catholic Church, Kabgayi, where we stayed for the rest of the genocide.

There were so many Tutsis in that compound, and the killers came each day and chose people to kill. I was lucky to be a child, because they weren't very interested in children. They were targeting adults to kill. That's where my mother died, and also where my brother died. They came each day and killed so many people, day by day. We stayed there until June 2, when the RPF liberated the area.

The living conditions were horrible there. There were thousands of people living in the camp without food or medicine. Thousands of people died from hunger or disease, because there was no way to get food or medication and no one was bringing it to us. I can't explain how bad the living conditions were then. For us to survive was only the will of God. You cannot imagine what it was like to go weeks with hardly any food and nothing to cover ourselves. This is why we should shout that God is really alive. When we say we know God, it's tangible. When we say we have seen God and that we know the miracles of God, we know what we are saying. I was so young, and I would go for three days at a time without eating or drinking. I did not survive by my own strength; it was truly a miracle. UNHCR [United Nations High Commission of Refugees] used to come once every three days to give children a biscuit. We would get one biscuit every three days, and then wait for them to come back. There were also some Hutu people living in the community who had good friends living in the church. They tried to get food to us, but we never knew who would come, or if they would come back to give us more food.

My brother was not killed by anyone, but he died due to the poor living conditions. He got sick, and couldn't get better and couldn't get any food, so he died. He was only three years old. My mother, brother, and I were all together, but once my brother got sick, they took him outside the camp, and they didn't allow my mother to go with him. There were some Hutus who cared about the refugees, and they were the ones to take my brother out. They took him to the hospital, but it was too late and so he died. We weren't able to bury him, and we don't know where he was buried.

My mother died later, when she was selected by the killers. The killers came to select people based on the length of the nose, height, and other characteristics common to Tutsis. This is how they chose my mother. I was with my mother when they came to take her away to die. When I saw them come to take her, I knew they were taking her to kill her, but I thought I would also die of starvation. I took it easily, because there was nothing I could do. I saw so many things happen and couldn't do anything. Life in Kabgayi was unbelievable. I stayed calm and waited to die. I thought tomorrow it could be me. There were many children like me who died in that camp. There were many people who went to sleep at night, who never woke up. They would go to sleep at night, and when you touched them in the morning, they had already died from hunger or disease. I didn't think I had a long time to live. The killers came and took people out of the church to kill them away from the camp. Those who resisted going with the killers were killed inside the church. They used spears, machetes, sticks, and other traditional weapons to kill people. The people who died in the church were not buried. Their bodies were taken and thrown in the forest, and the dogs ate their bodies. There was a terrible smell from all the bodies there. We saw all of this happening. During the genocide we saw dead people everywhere. Everywhere you moved you saw people who were killed. It became normal, because we even slept around the bodies and stayed with them. So we were not surprised to see people who had been killed everywhere. Things were catastrophic during this time; you cannot imagine how awful it was. We began to see it as normal, because we couldn't change anything. We thought it was how things had to be. I found out later that my uncle was also in that church, but it was such a large compound and so I didn't know that any of my family was there.

When the RPF came in, we saw they were different than the killers. The way they came and how they talked to us was different than what we knew. They told us they came to save us, but that there were still killers all around. They said they would show us the way to go, but that we needed to follow them and respect them and that no one could go their own way. They came in and had some simple medications to give to those who were very sick and transported those who couldn't walk by car. They showed us the direction to go, and we started going south. It was a long journey, and so we would stop to sleep, and then continue walking the next day. We traveled for almost one month. On the journey, the RPF gave us some food, but because of diseases, many people died. There were thousands of us making the journey. As we moved, different people joined us who had come from different places. Even Hutus who had not joined in the killings joined our group along the way. We would get somewhere for a night, but when the fighting came there, we would move again to another place that was safer. I saw so many dead people all around the road. I saw people walking, who would suddenly fall down. When I touched them, they were already dead. The war was all around us, so we could hear the sounds of the guns and shooting everywhere. After we got close to the border of Burundi and Rwanda, the RPF told us that all of Rwanda was safe [so we were able to stay in Rwanda, and did not cross the border]. It was the beginning of July [1994]. The RPF had stayed with us and protected us throughout the whole journey. After that, we stayed about one week there, near the border. We were told then that we were able to return to our home area and start our lives there. At that time, I was with my uncle and neighbor. I didn't know where my cousins and aunts were. We came back to Gitarama and spent days waiting for my aunts and cousins, to see if any had survived. After a few days, some of them returned as well.

After the genocide life was very difficult. Before the genocide I was with my mom and my brother. After, I was alone. I was the only survivor of my immediate family. I had some of my cousins and aunts and [an] uncle, but it was not easy for me. I was in despair. When I slept at night, I thought how bad the next day would be. I was not happy. I wanted to die, because living meant nothing to me. Life was not good then.

My cousins and I shared our pain with each other, and our extended family began to rebuild and try to make our lives better. An aunt brought me back to Kigali about two months after the genocide. I stayed there a long time, from primary two to primary five [second through fifth grades]. In primary five, I went back to Gitarama to live with my cousins and aunt and uncle there. In primary six [sixth grade], I went back to Kigali to live with another aunt in Nyamirambo. After two or three years, I decided to go and live with my aunt Julienne. Since I did not have parents, I wasn't able to have a stable life. One day I was at Nyamirambo, another in Gitarama, another in Kigali [living with different relatives].

Sometimes it was my choice to move, but sometimes it was not. Often it depended on the economic stability of my relatives and who could afford to have me live with them.

I lived like this, moving around a lot and in a state of emotional despair until 2000, when I received salvation. I was in senior one [seventh grade]. In secondary school [seventh through twelfth grades], there were gatherings for the whole school when pastors would come to preach to us. It was not a Christian school, but it was a private school and most of the people educated there were Christians. As a student I went because many of my classmates were going, and I wanted to see what was going on. The first time I didn't receive Jesus, but I went many times, and after about six times, I accepted Christ. Before receiving Christ, I was angry, and I wanted revenge. I was drinking a lot and smoking, and I wanted to die. I was desperate. When the pastor preached the gospel, I wanted the good life he talked about. I felt encouraged and when he called people to receive Jesus, I decided to do that to start a new beginning. I decided to change. On January 7, 2000, I was baptized. When I was saved, God's presence in my life helped to heal me. I learned that in God, I had value in Jesus. I had a new family of other Christians that were true friends. We sang songs of joy and hope together. We had pastors who preached and taught us the gospel. They encouraged us to stay in the church and have hope for the future. Emotionally, I felt so much better than before. I had hope, sang for joy, and was able to put all my strength into my education. I began to understand that a future was possible. I realized that I could live, that I could have hope for tomorrow.

After I received Christ, there were positive changes in me. I became more disciplined and more organized. I changed my actions, my relationships with friends, and I realized that my future was in my hands. I saw that I needed to orient myself towards a better future. I developed better character traits. I joined a choir and found good friends. I started a new journey. Although it was not easy, I left bad friends behind, even though they continued to pressure me to drink and smoke.

As the song says, "I have decided to follow Jesus/I have decided to follow Jesus/No turning back/No turning back."[4] So, I started a new journey and changed my negative aspects. The gospel message teaches us that, in Christ, we are a new creation. I learned that as a new creation, I could leave everything behind to follow Jesus. It gave me hope to know I could leave all the bad things from my past behind me to start a new life.

Forgiveness is a process. It's not something that happens once and finishes, or something that can take place in one day. Even if I could have revenge, I would not allow myself to. The word of God teaches us not to take revenge. I had no choice. To release myself, I had to forgive those who had killed. Forgiveness is an opportunity for me and for those people who have wronged me.

There are many changes in my life throughout the time after the genocide. I used to think I couldn't achieve anything, that I couldn't become anyone important, and that I didn't have value. Now, I feel proud of where I am and what I have achieved. In brief, from the start of secondary school [seventh grade] until now, I've done many things and had different opportunities. As I shared at the beginning of this interview, I'm a manager of a bank in Kigali. Before, I was nothing and I had nothing. I just dreamed about the future. Since starting secondary school, I put all my strength into my studies. I scored well on my national exams in secondary school, and I continued university studies and finished in finance and got a job. I am proud of what I have achieved, and I have value. Now I'm someone with a better present, and I have hope for the future.

I would like to emphasize to people the importance of believing in God. Americans have "In God We Trust" on dollar bills. Whatever

4   https://library.timelesstruths.org/music/I_Have_Decided_to_Follow_Jesus/

you do, know that God lives. As you read about my past tragedy and everything I went through, know that it's not by chance. My life is built by the grace of God. My life is built by the miracle of God. Know that there is something in control that is bigger than us— beyond our mind, beyond our everything. God is able. God is good.

The lessons I want to teach people is to believe in God, to respect God, and to love other people. Without love, you can't survive in this world. Love people, do good things for others, encourage others, and help people have hope for the future. Do not bring people down for who they are or what their life is like; respect them as they are. Respect people from different parts of the world, of different races, and of different ethnicities because we are all one body. We have different languages, different appearances, different economic statuses, and other things that separate us, but as people, we are still the same. Teach people to love each other. Make others proud. Thank you and God bless you.

[Elyse wished to share the following scripture from Colossians 1:10-12 as a part of his testimony.]

"Live a life worthy of the Lord and please Him in every way; bearing fruit in every good work, growing in the knowledge of God, being strengthened with all power according to His glorious might so that you may have great endurance and patience, and giving joyful thanks to the Father who has qualified you to share in the inheritance of His holy people in the kingdom of light."

CHAPTER 3:
YVETTE

Region: Bugesera/Nyamata

The van grinds to a halt in the gravel lot outside of mass graves at a church in Nyamata. Immediately, I feel the weight in the air pressing upon me, constricting my lungs; my voice stops in my throat. The chattering voices on the ride here, now still. Ben gets out of the van, and the other American women and myself follow his lead. We are here with him to try to grasp the reality of the atrocities committed during the genocide, and to better understand how we can partner alongside Ben in serving genocide survivors. In order to understand the needs of the present, we must confront the horrors of the past. The air heavy with the silence of thousands of voices that are eternally stilled, caught in time and space. Unspoken words, years, and lives left unlived fill the space from the van to the entrance of the church. My halting footsteps communicate my dread of what lays within, yet I am drawn forward nonetheless. As we are met by a solemn guide at the church doors, the history of Nyamata tragically unfolds in his quiet tones. My eyes adjust to the dim interior, confused at the piles of clothing I see covering the pews. "Victims' clothing." The guide's words cut through my unspoken questions. The House of God believed to protect and provide, turned into the perfect den for mass murder of the congregated Tutsis. Their clothing left where they were killed as a reminder.

Disembodied, my mind not able to keep up with what I'm seeing and hearing. My footsteps move toward the altar covered in rosaries, national identification cards, jewelry, personal items. I look up to see the Virgin Mother, intact on the wall, arm up, carefully watching over these valuables. Such loss of life under the unceasing vigil of The Mother, the carrier and protector of the ultimate life. My eyes are drawn toward brown splatters weaving in and out of items, covering the altar. "Blood," I hear, left where it was shed. The hypocrisy is paralyzing.

I follow our guide out of the sanctuary of death, holding the hand of the woman next to me, comforting her as she weeps. I am silent. My face is a stone, jaw unmoving, eyes dry. We are now stepping down below the church, into a room with a single coffin, guarded by a long metal pole. As I listen to the guide recounting the atrocious events that took place within these "sacred" walls, I try to take in the reality of what happened to the woman whose remains lie in the coffin before me.

"She was tortured. She was raped. She was murdered." The guide's words drift to me, cutting through my thoughts. The petite coffin holds a woman, captured by Hutu men, raped countless times, sexually tortured and mutilated. Conversations shift toward the metal pole, the instrument of her death. Driven up her vagina and through her internal organs, until it broke through the flesh, making its escape from the cavity of her body, allowing her to escape from the hell of life and enter the bliss of death.

My body is numb. The women I am with are all weeping now. Emotionally I feel numb, but I feel physically sick. I hold tightly and remain steady for those around me. My eyes can't fill. They are still dry. I know this is Yvette's auntie. I can only think of Yvette now: how does she feel coming here, seeing her auntie's coffin? Knowing her other family members lay here? I can't cry. What if this was my auntie?

I see Ben, our guide, with dry eyes. I want to cry for them, for their loss, for Yvette's loss. But I can't. So instead, I remain strong. I remain strong for them because I can't even begin to comprehend, to empathize, my life so safely nested away from the horrors of genocide.

My legs move forward, drinking in the sunshine as we emerge again. The church guide leads us around the back of the building. "Mass graves," he says, cutting into my consciousness. I look into the hole in the ground opening up before me and the steps that descend into the darkness. Ben grabs my hand and I look over to him.

"*Komera,*" he says. I nod, unable to open my mouth, assuring him I will be strong. I set my jaw. Some women choose to stay above the surface, but I know I can—I must—enter. Ben stays next to me as we descend into the pit, one step at a time. What nervousness I may have felt about what I would find is replaced by the strength provided to me by Ben's words.

Komera, I tell myself as my eyes adjust to the darkness. Rays of dust-filled sunlight somehow reach their tendrils into the depths. Shelves. Rows. Skulls. Femurs. Adults, children, infants. Bones. Intact, cracked, shattered. Bones.

Our guide explains the marks. The tales they tell of the type of death of the victims. Bones. Mothers. Fathers. Brothers. Sisters. Aunties. Uncles. Cousins. Friends. Loved ones. Lives unlived. Stories untold. Vibrant, full, loving, lives pregnant with potential. Reduced to bones.

As we emerge from the grave, my mind emerges to new levels of understanding, as I realize that those who lived lost more than those who died. As we walk back toward the van, I think of the survivors who lost everyone and everything, yet grasped tightly to life refusing to let go. Survivors who found a way to achieve life after death, the embodiment of *komera*, "to be strong." The van door slams as the engine starts. The word rolls around my tongue as I whisper it over to myself, forever embedded in my mind. *Komera*.

Bugesera and Nyamata are communities located in the eastern province. These are rural communities whose outskirts have access to the highway and are about a forty-five minute drive from Kigali.

Prior to genocide, the government had begun the strategic relocation of Tutsis. Bugesera and Nyamata were areas to which many Tutsis were forced to move.[5] The violence that preceded the genocide affected the area, and during such times many Tutsis would go to the Catholic church in Nyamata to seek refuge. During one of these times, an Italian nun living at Nyamata tried to bring the international world's attention to the ethnic issues in Rwanda. Afterward, she was killed by Hutu extremists. The government tried to cover up her murder and deny her accusations of ethnic discrimination.[6]

In 1994, many Tutsis fled to Nyamata Church during the genocide. It is estimated that forty-five thousand people were massacred there in one day. Today, Nyamata Church remains a memorial to genocide survivors. The pews of the church are covered in the clothes of the victims, and the altar is stained with their blood. In the back of the church is a memorial to the women who were raped and tortured during the genocide, and a plaque to commemorate a woman who suffered terrible sexual torture prior to her death. Outside the church, steps lead down into mass graves with shelves that hold the bones of the victims.

---

[5] http://kwibuka.rw/?memorial_sites=nyamata-memorial-site
[6] https://www.amnesty.org/download/Documents/196000/act790021992en.pdf

Yvette's family lived in Bugesera and Nyamata when the genocide began. Many of her extended family members died in Nyamata Church. Her aunt is the woman commemorated there who was brutally raped and tortured.

<u>VI: Yvette Uwase</u>

Name: Yvette Uwase
Year and place of birth: 1984, Bugesera
Age during genocide: nine
Family members killed during genocide: exact numbers are unknown; one sister, almost all extended family on her mother's side, all extended family on her father's side
Family members who survived genocide: mother, father, and three siblings
Schooling completed: secondary school [American equivalent of high school]
Occupation: stay-at-home mother, community member of Good News International, and the president of the choir, Voices of Good News
Currently living with: husband and three children
Language spoken for interview: Kinyarwanda; interpreted into English by Clement Ndayisaba

    Before genocide, my family lived at Nyamata. We had a good family, and I was the first born. Before genocide, there was a strategy the government used to limit schooling for Tutsis. Because of this, my father was a driver and didn't receive much education. At that time, a driver's license had value. It was like a degree, and so he was able to earn enough to support our family. Where we lived in Nyamata was near my mother's side of the family. My father's side of the family stayed in Ruhengeri, where we originally came from. We lived together with the other people in the community peacefully. People had good relationships with each other until the genocide started. In general, I can say that life before genocide was good, and the relationships with people were good.

About two years before the genocide things started changing, and I remember it very clearly. I was in primary three [third grade], and when I went to school the teachers made lists of Hutus and Tutsis. Sometimes, the teachers would have us stand and have Hutus go to one side of the classroom and Tutsis go to another. This is when I first realized there were different ethnic groups. I started to recognize the discrimination and bad relationships between these ethnic groups in 1992. I was staying with my auntie, who lived about ten minutes from Nyamata. I was living with my aunt, and I saw people fighting and burning other homes. There was an Italian nun living at Nyamata who was communicating with the international media and telling them that the government was killing Tutsis. This is when the Tutsi people started going to the Nyamata churches to hide. I realized things were changing. When this nun was telling the international community that people were being killed at Bugesera, the killers also killed her. After she died, many white people came in to investigate what had happened. Because the government was afraid of what would be discovered, they quickly quieted and calmed the situation, and had the people staying in the churches go back to their homes. After that, the area became peaceful again for a short period of time.

However, things continued to change. People were being taken to prison because they were accused of collaborating with the RPF. They took my father into prison at that time, saying he was a part of the RPF. I saw many things changing, but I was young and didn't fully understand what was happening, and so I didn't focus on it much. There were many Tutsis living near us at Bugesera, due to the government's strategy to relocate Tutsis there. Most of our community was Tutsi.

Our extended family had good relationships with each other.

Sometimes, different children would go and live with different families. At that time, my sister had gone to Ruhengeri to stay with my father's family, and I was living with my auntie about ten minutes from my parents. My father was still working as a driver for Doctors Without Borders. He was home sometimes, but spent most of his time working for them. Because I was living with my auntie, my parents and siblings often came to visit us. There was always a lot of movement and visiting. We were a very close family. All my family members were Christians, and we went to the Catholic church. Before the genocide started, we were preparing to celebrate my baptism. I was planning to be baptized on Easter.

I remember the day the genocide started. It started on a Wednesday, which was a market day. That day, I didn't go to school. A few days before the genocide started, my mother was sick, and my auntie went to visit her. When she got there, she saw she was not doing well. She went to the bus station to send someone to tell my father, because he usually didn't come home until Friday. The message reached my father, and he came home that day. When he came, he stayed with my mom overnight. The next day, he came to my auntie and bought medicine from the pharmacy. He gave me the medicine to bring to my mom. After my father bought the medicine, my aunt asked me to hurry and give it to her and then come back soon, because she was busy and needed my help with the little children. When I got home, I found my mom very sick. We had people at home who were helping us, but I didn't want to leave my mom alone. I decided not to go back [to my auntie's], but to stay with my mom.

That day I stayed with my mom, was the day President Habyarimana was killed. The next day was different, and I couldn't leave the house to go back [to my auntie's]. There were not many Interahamwe militia where we were living, but there were many people who knew my family who were coming to my home. In Nyamata, closer to where my auntie lived, there were many

Interahamwe who had begun killing. There were people from that area coming to our home for safety. They had started killing at Nyamata, but we were still safe at our house. After four days, we were still safe at home. However, we heard that Tutsis were being killed in many other places.

On the fifth day, things changed. They attacked our home, and we decided to leave and join others who were trying to find a safe place to be. We had a lot of food, because it was harvest time. Before we left home, we cooked lots of food to take with us. That night, we went to Ntarama school. At night, we could see the mountain where our homes were, and we saw our homes being burned. The Interahamwe found out that many Tutsis had gone to that school to hide. The next day, they came to start killing people there. I can't remember the dates well, but the killers came every day to kill people. My uncles saw that soon we would be killed, and so they decided to lead the family to cross the Nyabarongo river to get into the south province of Rwanda. At that time, I was with my mom, sisters, two uncles, and two people who worked for my family. We decided to leave the school, and we all went to the river. Some of the people by the river were killers. My uncle was with his fiancé. They decided that the men should go first, to see what the other side was like. So, my uncles went first in the boat, but when they got into the boat, the killers took one of my uncles who was very tall, and threw him into the river. We didn't see it happen, but my uncle who survived told us how it happened after the genocide. The people who were working for our family were Hutu, but they were still with us. When we realized our uncles weren't coming back to take us to the other side of the river, we decided to go back to the school. We were with my young[er] brother, who was three months old, and my mother who was still sick. So, we decided to go back immediately. We stayed at the school at night, but during the day we moved into the bushes to hide.

One day, there were many people who decided to stay at the school during the day, because killers were also coming to the bushes. My sisters and I went back to the bushes, but because my mother was sick, she stayed in the school. That day, the killers had organized themselves and brought more Interahamwe on buses to come and kill. The Hutu people who worked for our family decided to leave, because it had gotten so dangerous. I had to take responsibility, since my uncles had been killed and my mother was sick. I woke up my mother, got my young sisters, and we left. I think it was a message from God telling me to take my sisters and mom because a short time after we left, we heard the noises of guns and grenades as they killed people. All of the people who had stayed in the church were killed that day. I would guess there were about four hundred people, but it's hard to say because people were inside and outside around the church. Most of my mom's family stayed there, and that's where they died. We moved down to the bushes, but there were Interahamwe who were shooting and killing people in the bushes. God protected us until we could get into the valley farther away and hide ourselves in the bushes. Because the killers were tired after all the killing in the church, they didn't come into the bushes to find more people. During the night, some people went back to the church to find survivors. They took those who had survived out from among the dead bodies and put them all into one room. I stayed with my sisters in the bushes while this was going on. We were close enough to hear people crying, which is how we knew there were survivors, and we could see the blood of people everywhere. I saw the bodies of people who had been killed. We were hiding about a five minute walk away. When my mother went back to the church, she found three of her cousins still alive, but with many wounds. She also found her mom, but she was about to die, because she had machete wounds all over her back. My mom took my cousins into another room to care for them. Yesterday, I just went to a wedding that was for one of these cousins.

Since our family was in different parts of Rwanda, we tried to get information about what was going on in other areas while we were hiding around the school. We learned that some of my aunties and my grandfather had been killed.

So many people were afraid to be with us, because it was difficult to hide with children. When they were hungry, sometimes young children would cry and then the killers would find them. People advised my mom to separate us, so that we had different hiding spots in the bushes, so that if the killers came, we would not all be killed at the same time. I don't remember well, but I would estimate we spent about three weeks there.

After three weeks, there was not any more food there, so my mom decided to take us back to our home area. We went back, and found our houses destroyed. We lived near our homes at night, and during the day went back to hide in the bush. It was [the] rainy season, and we had to stay outside overnight. When it rained, we had no way to protect ourselves from the rain, and so it was a bad life. My mom was still sick, but she did her best to do everything to care for us. It was myself, and my three other siblings together. My father and other sibling[s] were not with us. We used to go to the bushes early in the morning, but she didn't listen to the advice to separate us-we stayed together in the bushes. It was difficult to get to the bushes, because it was far from our home.

One time, we were going from the bushes to the home, but we didn't make it there and spent the night outside on the way to the house. That night, we decided we couldn't go back to the bushes, or continue because it was starting to get light. We stayed in the sorghum bushes that were nearby. We were sitting in the sorghum bushes, which were next to the banana trees near our home. We heard people taking bananas off our tree, but we didn't know if they were killers or others, so we stayed quiet so they wouldn't know that we were there. When we were listening to those people talking, my young[er] sister was hungry and started crying. We took the soil and put it in her mouth to try to keep her quiet. She didn't stay quiet, and the people heard us and started shouting, saying that there were Tutsis hiding in the sorghum bushes. There was one man, and two younger people. They stopped cutting down the bananas, and immediately came into the sorghum bushes. My mom took my young[er] sister and started running. There was another mother with a young baby who also ran with my mother. I stayed in the sorghum bush with my other sisters. Immediately after my mom started running, I stood up to follow her. We couldn't follow them, because there was a man near us with a machete. The man saw me stand up and was coming toward us. I decided to run, because the other children were sleeping. Since I was older, I chose to run, and the man ran after me. He wanted to catch me and kill me. When I got tired, I had to stop. I was so traumatized because he was going to kill me, and so I said, "Please forgive me and I will show you where my mother went." I said that very loudly, and some other people heard. Today when I meet people who heard that, they remind me of what I said. Even though I said that, I didn't know where my mother was, and I only said it because I was traumatized. When he got to me, he immediately cut me with the machete, and I fell down. He thought that I was dead, and so he left me. He left and went back where I was, and found my sister and my brother who had stayed there. He started cutting them with his machete as well, and he also left them for dead. They were so hungry and tired, they didn't make any sound. I was alone, they were alone, and my mom was separated with my youngest sister. I felt like I had died, because I was so afraid. We had seen many people who were killed, and I had so much fear when I saw the killers, because I knew what they could do and how they killed people. I was lying down, but I was not far from my sister and brother.

Eventually, my sister woke up, and took my young[er] brother over to where I was, and they woke me up. They were calling my name, and I woke up and saw my head was bleeding from where I was cut with machetes. I couldn't move, but they helped me go back into the sorghum bushes. When we went back where we were hiding, we saw that the man had taken the clothes and food we had there. There was nothing left. We stayed there, and in the evening my mom came to see what happened to us. She came back to the bushes, and she was happy to see we were still alive. She thought we had been killed, and she came to see if we had died to bury our bodies. She came and was surprised to see we were still alive. Even though we were still alive, since we were all cut, it was difficult for us to move with our wounds. She took us to a different place to hide in the sorghum bushes. We found other people who were still alive who used traditional medicine to make sure our wounds didn't get infected. Since we weren't able to go far, we didn't go back into the valley and we stayed in the sorghum bushes. The other survivors we met in the bushes were also from our community.

When we were in the bushes, we saw another car with the Interahamwe killers. When they saw the bushes, they stopped to check and see if anyone was there. By chance, they went to the other side of the bushes, but they didn't come to the part we were hiding in. We kept so quiet that we didn't even breathe, so that they would not hear any noise. We saw them moving all around with their machetes, sticks, and guns, but since they didn't find anyone, they went back to their car and they left. During that time, I couldn't think about anything. My mind was blank, and I felt like I died. We stayed there and slept there, and didn't even know when they left, we were so afraid. Since there were so many people, the other times the Interahamwe came, they found other people in the other side of the sorghum bushes. After they killed them, they left. We kept living in this way. People were dying every day. Some were lucky to not be killed, but so many died each day. We stayed in the sorghum bushes two days after we were cut with machetes.

It became more dangerous after those two days, because the RPF soldiers were fighting nearby. The killers were trying to do their job of killing quickly, because they knew the RPF were coming. The killers were around every day killing people in the bushes because they were afraid the RPF would chase them away before they could finish killing everyone. My mother continued to encourage us by telling us we would survive and that our father would survive, even though we didn't know where he was. In addition to this, I became sick. We were very vulnerable during that time. When I was sick, the killers saw us and were coming to kill us. When the killers came, they found another family before they got to us. While they were busy killing that other family, we moved to another hiding place.

On the last day, all of the killers went into the bushes. They decided to kill everyone by burning the bushes. They set the bushes on fire, so that no one would survive. We were in the bush nearby, but they went and burned the bushes below us. They didn't burn the bushes where we were, because they knew many people were hiding in the bushes below us. We saw the smoke and heard the noise of the fire and the people trying to run. That evening, the RPF came to that place and looked for survivors. After about four days, the RPF found us and took us from there. Some people had serious wounds, but they took all the survivors from the area to Nyamata. They encouraged us to not be afraid, because they were going to help. They gave us food and water and helped us start a new life. The RPF had taken control of that area, but the genocide was still going on in other places. Some of the soldiers stayed to protect us, but others went to fight the killers in other places. My auntie had lived in Nyamata and we wanted to get information about her. After some time, we went to her home to see what we could find. When we got there, we didn't find anything in the house, and the house was destroyed. We didn't find her body, so we didn't know if she was killed or not.

We continued to try to get information about the people in our family who were killed. We found out that two uncles and one auntie survived. As the area became safer, we moved around to see if we could find people who had died. We found the clothes of my uncle near a water tank, but we couldn't find him. When we looked in the water tank, we saw that they had killed him and thrown him in the water tank. It was not only him; there were also others who were killed and thrown in the water tank. Soldiers protected us and helped us find the bodies of our family members. When we got to the home of one of the Interahamwe, we found so many peoples' bodies, including the bodies of many people in our family who were killed in his home. We found them, and took their bodies in sheets to a church, because we didn't want them left everywhere.

All that time we were not with my father. My father had found his way to Burundi, and he joined the RPF that was there. He drove cars for them. He heard that we were still alive, and so he left the army to come and find us. He found us at Nyamata and then took us to Kigali. As we moved around, we couldn't find any information about my auntie, but when we got to Kigali, my father learned about my auntie and where she was killed. We learned that she was raped before she was killed, and she was tortured. We don't know the number who raped her, but we were told it was so many people. When we found her, she had a stick that was driven up her vagina, and we found her baby who she was killed with. Her baby was three months old during the genocide, and was the same age as my youngest sibling at that time. The government decided to take her body to the memorial at Nyamata church to remember and to show people what happened to women during the genocide. We were not happy to see her body there, and we asked the government to bury her privately, and they agreed to let us do so. We wrote a book about my auntie's life, and how she was killed, although the book is not yet published. We are trying to find people to sponsor publishing the book so that people can learn about her life and what happened to women during the genocide, but it's still an ongoing project.

During that time, we already knew about almost everyone in our family, except my sister who was living in Ruhengeri. When people brought me clothes, I would keep clothes for her, hoping that one day I would see her. It was two months after the genocide when my father decided to go to Ruhengeri to see what had happened to his family and see if anyone was alive. When he got there, he found that everyone had been killed. There was no one who survived. My sister died there with them. They are buried in the memorial site there.

After the genocide, we continued with life, but we had no hope because we had lost so many people in our family. We wondered if we would ever really live again. My father found another job driving a minister's car, and we went back to our studies. We started finding a new life. I finished my primary studies [first through sixth grades] and went to secondary school [grades seven to twelve]. The survivors' fund helped pay for our education. Because I was the first born, I was responsible for many things at home. After the genocide, my parents had four more children, so now there were eight children in the family. I didn't continue studying, because I had to help my mom because I was oldest. I missed class so many times to come and help the family. When my mother was giving birth, I had to come home to care for the children and care for her. Our life conditions were bad. We spent a lot of time thinking about those who had died, and I was always unhappy. I couldn't see anything good. I felt very negative, although I never thought negatively about God. Even though all those people were killed, my parents and many of my brothers and sisters survived. I knew I was lucky because many people I saw had lost their brothers, sisters, and parents. Many people had lost everyone. I knew I was lucky to still have them.

When I was in senior five [eleventh grade], I decided to get married because of all the challenges and responsibilities I had. It was too early for me, but because of the conditions of life, I had no choice. I got married, and I'm now living with my husband and my children. After I got married, I started to have happiness. I'm lucky to have my mother-in-law, because she is a very good woman and cares for me. They have a family because they had been living in Bujumbura, Burundi during the genocide. They are good people, and it's been good for me to be with them and be able to join their family. I was twenty-three when I got married and started a new life of happiness.

Now, I have hope for the future. My brothers and sisters are growing up well, and my parents have returned to our home area. My father is no longer a driver and he stays at home with my mom. I have a good family, and we go to see them often.

My spiritual and emotional healing started when I got baptized in the Pentecostal church in 1999. Jesus gave me many promises, but I still was not following Him fully, and I did not feel like I could hear His voice. In August of 2013, my son was sick for a long time, and there were many people who came to my home to pray for him. When they prayed for him and shared the word of God with us is when I received Jesus fully. I truly experienced Jesus coming into my heart and I decided to follow Him. I realized that there was a reason why I survived and that I had to work for Him.

There have been so many changes since then, because I started loving and reading the Bible. I realized that God loved me. I learned how the children of Adam had killed one another, and I realized that what had happened in the genocide had happened before with the people of God. I saw that it was the devil's plan, but that Jesus was victorious. I learned that the devil never wins, and that the plans of God will prevail.

The lesson I want to teach others is only about love. If there is love between people, if people would love their neighbors as they love themselves, they couldn't make the decision to kill one another. I encourage people to love one another and keep the law of love. As Jesus said, we need to love our neighbors as we love ourselves. Since we were created in love and loved by God, we also need to love one another.

[Yvette requested the following Bible verses from John 1:1-18 be included with her testimony].

"In the beginning was the Word, and the Word was with God, and the Word was God. He was with God in the beginning. Through him all things were made; without him nothing was made that has been made. In him was life, and that life was the light of all mankind. The light shines in the darkness, and the darkness has not overcome it.

"There was a man sent from God whose name was John. He came as a witness to testify concerning that light, so that through him all might believe. He himself was not the light; he came only as a witness to the light.

"The true light that gives light to everyone was coming into the world. He was in the world, and though the world was made through him, the world did not recognize him. He came to that which was his own, but his own did not receive him. Yet to all who did receive him, to those who believed in his name, he gave the right to become children of God—children born not of natural descent, nor of human decision or a husband's will, but born of God.

"The Word became flesh and made his dwelling among us. We have seen his glory, the glory of the one and only Son, who came from the Father, full of grace and truth.

"John testified concerning him. He cried out, saying, 'This is the one I spoke about when I said, "He who comes after me has surpassed me because he was before me."' Out of his fullness we have all received grace in place of grace already given. For the law was given through Moses; grace and truth came through Jesus Christ.

"No one has ever seen God, but the one and only Son, who is himself God and is in closest relationship with the Father, has made him known."

CHAPTER 4:
MARY JANE

Region: Rugalika

I bounce alongside Ben and Scholastique as he winds the truck around the potholes and hills of the dirt roads on our way to a gathering of widows within the Good News community outside of Kigali. We come to a dusty stop and are instantly surrounded by warm greetings of "*Mwiriwe, Amakuru*" that gently glide through the warm air. The truck is surrounded before the engine shudders to a stop. Doors slam and my feet hit the red dirt. Guiding me, Scholastique grabs my hand.

Other hands clasp in greeting with one another and cheeks touch in respect and care. One, two, three—I carefully count the number of touches. My arm is clasped just above the elbow, and ever so slightly, I nod my head in respect to those I'm greeting. My eyes watch Scholastique. I mimic the ways of the Rwandan women as seamlessly as I can, all the while knowing the hue of my skin will never allow me to meld into the culture around me. White, purple, yellow, and pink flowers burst with fragrance, slowly float off the trees down to the dusty road, and overwhelm my senses with beauty. They're quickly trampled into a dusty reddish brown. My gaze rises to meet that of the woman across from me. Her dark chocolate eyes are soft, deep, full of wisdom, and strong with a love that has been refined through the fires of pain.

Scarred and once broken in body, heart, and spirit, these women now walk with new life in their steps, as we-Scholastique, Ben, and I-follow the crowd into a local church for a gathering. I pass through the doorway and the greetings continue from those who arrived before us. Machete wounds that never fully healed mark the arms that stretch out in loving welcome as the community congregates. I feel unworthy to be in the midst of women of such poise, resilience, and character, ever aware of my privilege and opportunity. My plain western clothing contrasts sharply with the kaleidoscopic beauty of *ikitenge* that adorn women arriving from their homes, fields, and blended families. The church fills to capacity.

We are taking part in a gathering of mostly women and orphans who have survived the genocide. The group is inside a church set in the hills of rural Rwanda and everyone is singing in Kinyarwanda. I can't understand the words, but the emotion and the body language speak straight to my heart. I can feel the joy, gratitude, love, and unity.

How can wounded hands stretch up and out, palms open and hearts softened, to receive peace and extend comfort? I marvel at the miracle of how those who have narrowly escaped death and witnessed their loved ones' murders can lift their voices up in thanksgiving to God. Honored to be in their presence, I ponder these thoughts. My eyes drift out the paneless windows to the singing birds, and emerald, rolling hills studded with banana trees. The women transition from singing hymns, to sharing their personal stories of how they survived the genocide. One woman speaks at a time, while the rest listen in respectful and understanding silence. Voices laced with pain bring my mind back into the room, and to the quiet whispering of Scholastique who fills the sounds with meaning, as she interprets for me. My mind and ears are now at capacity. There is no place for the stories to enter but into my heart.

Story after story slowly, painfully unfolds, as memories filled with the darkness and suffering of the past excruciatingly surface from the depths of the minds where they had been carefully hidden—hidden, yet never forgotten. While the details of the pain and suffering vary, the miracle of life within each survivor's story shines brightly. I witness beauty unfold as the clouds of darkness lift from the eyes of the speaker.

As stories are shared, hearts are opened, while the reality of pain is simultaneously met with hope for the future. The eyes of those who voice their unfathomable suffering radiate hope and healing as they share their stories. The speaker is surrounded and showered with tears and empathy. They come together to strengthen, to comfort, to encourage-hugging, singing, praying. In awe, I am brought back to the present and find my own eyes brimming with tears.

The rural community Rugalika is less than an hour's drive from Kigali. Winding dirt roads make access to parts of the area difficult, while other parts are located near the main highway and are more accessible.

Rugalika joined Good News International in 2013. Women who lived in Rugalika requested a Good News staff member visit the genocide survivors in the area to encourage them and advise them how to best rebuild their lives. Upon the arrival of myself, Ben, and his youngest daughter Tianna (age ten at the time), approximately thirty female genocide survivors and an additional ten or so of orphan-headed households had gathered to welcome us. The group said they were not looking for any money, but rather, what they most wanted were people to bring them hope and encouragement.

In light of their abject poverty, this request highlighted their deep needs for emotional and spiritual healing. Their leader said that they had not received any emotional or spiritual counseling since 1994. This community is unique in its self-advocacy and awareness of needs.

In 2014, I went to visit Rugalika with Good News International to do a group counseling session. During this session, a woman named Mary Jane stood up to share her testimony. Pulling up her sleeves and rolling down her collar to reveal the scars left on her neck and arms, Mary Jane shared how, at the age of fourteen, she miraculously survived the killers' machetes. During her brief, yet poignant testimony, my eyes met hers and then followed her to her seat. I was driven to learn more about the joy and hope this woman had twenty years after being orphaned. I sought her out after the gathering, and Mary Jane graciously granted my request to share more of her experiences. Patiently, she walked with me for nearly thirty minutes to a dusty soccer field and waited, while our translator organized the youth of the community to begin a game. Due to the unexpected nature of this interview we had limited, yet meaningful time.

VII: Mary Jane

Name: Mary Jane
Year and place of birth: 1980, Kamonyi District
Age during genocide: fourteen
Family members killed during genocide: mother, father, six brothers, and two sisters
Family members who survived genocide: none
Schooling completed: primary three [American equivalent of third grade]
Occupation: agriculture
Currently living with: two children
Language spoken for interview: Kinyarwanda; interpreted into English by Clement Ndayisaba

Mary Jane rolls up her sleeves, exposing pale lines running parallel on her arms. Turning, her gentle fingers need not point to the scars permanently disfiguring her neck. Her eyes meet mine. I can hardly believe the quiet words emerging from her lips. Brutalized by her neighbors. Left for dead. Lying in pools of blood surrounded by bodies. The hot sun rising and setting on her body, barely alive. Rescued, recovered, only to return to the very community and neighbors that hunted her family. Not only forgiveness, but reconciliation. Former murderers, turned neighbors again. She helps them, and they help her in the absence of her own family.

Pushing myself up from the ground, shaking the dust off my hands, reaching out to hug this phenomenal woman. *"Murakoze cyane,"* I say, offering my inadequate thanks, longing to put to words all that my heart feels. How can I ever express appropriate gratitude for what I've just learned? My mind reels. A welcome breeze brings slight relief from the blazing sun. I gaze with admiration on her small frame, marveling at her strength. She leaves and becomes indistinguishable in a group that melds into one form before disappearing into the distance. Clement is packed and patiently waiting for me. I rush to gather the rest of my things, realizing that all the others are already waiting in the truck.

Before the genocide we had a family of eleven, including my siblings and my parents. We had a good life, as my parents worked in agriculture, and we always had enough food. They were able to sustain us through agriculture, and we had everything that we needed. My family had good relationships with our neighbors, and we were a family without any economic, or other problems. Our family was safe in our community, and we had many friends. My family and I were Christians, and we went to a Catholic church in our community. We had everything that we needed.

I first learned about ethnic groups two years before genocide [at age twelve] when I went to school. We all went to school, and there we learned we were a mixed group of children; Hutus and Tutsis went to school together. Teachers would say, "Tutsis stand up," and they gave us different seats. Then they would say, "Hutus stand up," and they would give them different seats. So I learned about different ethnic groups from teachers in the classrooms.

We used to have a place where we would meet as children to play games. Then when genocide started, I was at that place playing with other children. As we were playing, I saw people I knew from church, and I noticed that most of the men were carrying machetes, spears, and sticks. I didn't know what was happening or what to do.

Then I saw my neighbors running away, because the men were doing bad things to them. At that time, I was still confused and couldn't think much of anything, because I wasn't aware of what they were going to do. Later, my parents told me they were coming to kill us, and then I was afraid they would kill me, too. After that time, the killing started. Before they started to kill, they first came to destroy the Tutsi houses of my family and our neighbors.

My family ran away, but they came behind us to kill us. At the same time, they caught my family and other Tutsis and gathered us all together. They started with my parents, and they killed them. After my parents, they killed my brothers. Then they killed my sisters. They killed my whole family with machetes. Then they came to me and cut me with machetes. I was fourteen years old. Because I fell down, they thought I'd died, because my whole family was laying down dead. I was cut with machetes on my neck, head, and arms. The killers didn't know I was still alive. I laid there for two days. I can't remember much of anything from those two days, because it was like I was dead. I remember that I was hungry and thirsty, and I was so hot from the sun. Because of fear I was in another state of mind, and I couldn't think much of anything. I was like a person who was dead. At that time I was a Christian, and before genocide I was in Sunday school. While I was lying on the ground, I was praying for God to help me, and I was praying that if I was killed, that I would be taken to heaven.

During the two days I laid there on the ground, and during that time others were brought to that place to be killed. After two days of lying in the sun, the Red Cross came to look for survivors. I was making small movements with my body because of my hunger and thirst, and because of my movement the Red Cross members found me. They took me, and the others they found alive, to a hospital. I stayed in the hospital for two months until the genocide was finished.

While I was in the hospital, I was healed from the physical wounds caused by the machetes, but I was mentally and emotionally traumatized. I thought of my family every day, and I kept remembering the way that they were killed. At one point when I was in the hospital, I thought God was not alive because he took my family. I thought, 'God if you took my family to heaven, please protect me and bring me there too.' But even when I was in the hospital and questioning God, I realized God had protected me, and that He loved me.

After the genocide I had no one who had survived from my family. Before the genocide I was in primary three [third grade], but after the genocide I was unable to continue school due to the wounds I suffered from the machetes on my neck, head, and arms.

I went back to my home area, because I didn't know what else to do. I didn't find anything there, and didn't find anyone. I went to a friend of my family's house and stayed there for a little time. Then I moved to another friend's house. I continued like this, moving all around with different people.

The first step towards healing I took was when God showed me that whatever happened He's still God in my life. God taught me to forgive people and for life to continue no matter what had happened. I prayed, and through the Word of God He showed me that He sent His son, Jesus, as a sacrifice. If Jesus came to forgive everyone, how could I not forgive? I learned from the Word of God to forgive as I had been forgiven.

I have met face to face the people who killed my family. They came to me to repent, and to ask for forgiveness. I felt God pushing me to forgive them. I still live in the same community as those who killed my family, and I live at peace with them. When I don't have water they give water to me, and when they don't have water I give water to them. They are my neighbors, and we help each other.

The lesson I would like to teach all those who hear my testimony is that even though I passed through a difficult period, I learned that nothing is greater than God. God protected me, and He allowed my life to continue after genocide. The second lesson I want people to know is that God heals wounded hearts. No matter what problems and challenges people face in their lives, and no matter what hurts people have, God is able to heal wounds and resolve problems. The last thing I want to tell people is that all humans are all created in the image of God. We need to respect one another and see each other as equals. We cannot separate or divide ourselves, for God loves each one of us.

CHAPTER 5:
INNOCENT, ALPHONSE, FABIAN

Region: Bisesero

Located in the Western province of Rwanda, Bisesero is a small, rural, community tucked into the hills. Hours of slow driving on winding, bumpy, dirt roads inhibit access to the area. Breathtaking views of Lake Kivu and the cool climate that is provided by the altitude of the region make it one of the most stunning areas of Rwanda.

Bisesero is known for its unique genocide history. Prior to genocide, this area was heavily populated by Tutsis, making it a target for Interahamwe during the genocide. After April 7, 1994, the Tutsi community banded together under the leadership of Aminadabu Birara and formed a resistance on the highest mountain in the area. They fought back the killers using traditional weapons such as spears and stones. There were many caves on the mountain, in which men hid their wives and children during the fighting. This group became the most successful resistance of the genocide.

The resistance remained successful until French soldiers came to the area promising deliverance for the Tutsis.. After the French had gathered nearly all the Tutsis in the area into one large group they left for three days. Buses of Interahamwe roared up to the group of Tutsis and the slaughter began. Complete chaos ensued as men, women, and children fled, while the Interahamwe came through mercilessly killing all they could reach. Many who fled and hid in caves were followed and burned alive. Those who ran back to the mountain were also soon defeated. It is estimated that over forty thousand Tutsis were killed in the Bisesero region, and less than 1,500 Tutsis survived.[7,8]

Due to the resistance in this area, there are more male survivors here than in other parts of the country. In addition, the betrayal from the French caused distrust of foreigners—they are a close-knit community that is wary to let strangers in. As a result, the following testimonies were gathered through written questionnaires. The Good News leader of the region, Fabian, asked community members Innocent and Alphonse to share their stories. Fabian is a member of the Mubuga community, and oversees all the Good News communities in the Kibuye area. Mubuga is within the greater Bisesero area, and thus his written testimony is included in this segment, as much of the history of the area is the same. The testimonies were written in notebooks, and then sent back to the Good News headquarters through Fabian. Their writing was then translated verbally into English, and finally transcribed in English.

---

[7] https://www.hrw.org/reports/1999/rwanda/Geno4-7-02.htm
[8] http://kwibuka.rw/?memorial_sites=bisesero-memorial-site

VIII: Innocent Kagorora

Name: Innocent Kagorora
Year and place of birth: 1981, Bisesero, Karongi District, Western Province
Age during genocide: thirteen
Family members killed in genocide: Seven immediate family members
Family members who survived genocide: two immediate family members
Schooling completed: secondary school [American equivalent of high school]
Occupation: unemployed
Currently living with: lives alone
Language used for interview: written in Kinyarwanda and interpreted into English by Clement Ndayisaba

Before the genocide I lived in a village called Jugewe in Bisesero in the western province. There were eight children in my family, and we all lived with our parents. Our parents were farmers and they cultivated to get food for the family. We lived in harmony and were at peace with our neighbors. We visited one another, participated in weddings for people of both ethnic groups, went to ceremonies for one another, and we were Christians. We attended the Seventh Day Adventist Church. Christianity taught us to respect God and to respect our colleagues and our friends. That's what the word of God taught us and encouraged us to do. We all lived in peace. We lived in love with our neighbors and we all believed in one God and in Jesus our savior.

Before genocide, we had three different ethnic groups: Hutu, Tutsi, and Twa. When I was a child I didn't know about the different ethnicities. I first learned about the ethnic groups in 1992 when people started to be separated by their group, and when it became more dangerous for Tutsis. In 1992 the political parties began to be more active. There were political parties that taught people to segregate and discriminate by ethnicity. That's when I learned our family was Tutsi. People changed a lot between the time when I was born until 1994, and there was so much anger and hatred. I saw all of this happening, but because I was young I didn't understand everything that was going on or know how intense it would become. I was thirteen years old in 1994, and by then I knew what was happening was bad, and I had seen how much people had changed.

The genocide started on April 7, 1994. Early in the morning we got the message that the father of the country had died. They were talking about the president, Habyarimana. At that time, the Hutus started preparing their machetes and spears, and started to mobilize by singing songs about killing the Tutsis. They said that the president had been killed by a Tutsi. We made groups in our community, with the Tutsis on one side and the Hutus on another side. People no longer had any relationship with each other. The next day people were coming to our house and to our neighbors. Before they killed us, they came and took our possessions and killed our cows. We saw it had become very dangerous. We decided to go far away and hide so they couldn't kill us. We went to hide on a mountain near our home. There were not many Hutu living in our area, so they called the Interahamwe killers from other western districts to come to Bisesero. Many Tutsis had gathered on that mountain, and so when the Interahamwe came, we started to fight back against the killers. We were able to resist, and we fought the killers for two months.

At the beginning of June in 1994, the French soldiers came to the area and called all the Tutsis out of hiding [from] the mountains and the forests. They told us that they were going to protect us, and that no one would be killed anymore. After they came, they told us they were going to stay with us, and that they would protect us so that nothing more would happen to us. However, on the third day, the French soldiers left. That's when the killers came in and killed almost everyone. When the killers first came to our home at the beginning of the genocide, my whole family escaped. But on that day when the French soldiers abandoned us, seven of my family members were killed. Only my sister, my brother, and I survived. We survived because when they started killing, we immediately ran away. Because they were busy killing so many people, one after the other, they were not able to stop everyone. When we ran, we went back into the bushes, where we lived day and night. During the time when we were in the bushes and the forest, I was shot in the shoulder. Because I was not able to move, the killers came to where I was lying. They started beating me with sticks to see if I was still alive. They thought I was dead, so they left without killing me. We stayed in the bushes until the RPF came in and took those who were still alive to Gitarama. When the RPF came, I was still injured from being shot and beaten. I was taken to the hospital, but because I had gone so long without any treatment, I was very sick. When I was at the hospital, I didn't have any hope of being healed or continuing with life. During that time, I thought a lot and had many questions about God. Because I was thirteen, I knew that God had loved people, but the killers had told us that our God had left us. I believed that God was no longer there, and that He had rejected us. I didn't think there was anyone to care for us.

After the genocide I was an orphan. My parents, five brothers and sisters, and many members of my extended family were all killed. We were too young to live on our own, and so I was taken to an orphanage in Kibuye. Due to my injuries, I was not strong enough physically to live on my own, but my sister and brother were older than me, and they were able to live on their own. They wanted me to go to the orphanage because I was injured, but since living conditions at the orphanage were bad, they wanted to try to find a better quality of life. We did not want to all die together at the orphanage, so we decided to separate. They went back to our home area where our house used to be, in Bisesero. After I got to the orphanage, I was taken to different hospitals because my injuries were so bad. They even took me to a hospital in Goma, in the Democratic Republic of the Congo. When I got back from Goma, I found that the orphanage had been moved from Kibuye to Gitarama. Once I got to the new orphanage in Gitarama, I found other members of my extended family who had survived the day the French left us at Bisesero. I stayed in the orphanage until 1997, which is when I went back to school for the first time. I started in primary four [fourth grade], finished primary [sixth grade], and started secondary school [seventh through twelfth grade]. I was studying economics and accounting, but I was not able to continue my university studies because I did not have money to pay for school. During those years, I struggled in many ways. As orphans, there was no one to help us and no one to care. I struggled with the other orphans to find ways to survive.

There have been many consequences of the genocide. The genocide left me handicapped, and I still suffer from the injuries I got during the genocide. Another consequence is that I am an orphan. I have had to live most of my life without many members of my family, and I haven't had the opportunity to be around family and to be happy. We live like we were born alone, with no family. We don't have people who can give us advice, because we've lost most of our parents. We don't have older people to care and to help us orient and direct our lives.

Overall, the Gacaca courts were really helpful. Of course, there were many challenges, as many people pretended to tell the truth. Some people only told part of the truth of what they had done, and some told lies. [Due to the large number of killers during the genocide, the traditional justice and prison system within Rwanda was unable to handle the capacity of people that had committed murder. As a result, the Gacaca courts were born. These courts were gatherings led by judges elected by the community, and did not have prior judicial experience. During the courts, genocide perpetrators were called forward to confess their crimes, and asked forgiveness from any surviving family members of their victims. After the confession and request for forgiveness, most of the people who had committed murder during the genocide returned to their homes and lived in their communities with those who had survived. While some accepted this, the courts left a mixed legacy, and many survivors were unhappy with the release of defendants and the lack of reparations. The Gacaca courts were used throughout Rwanda from 2005 through 2012 to bring justice, foster reconciliation within communities, and to shed the light of truth upon the atrocities of the genocide. The courts processed an estimated two million cases during this time period. Gacaca courts, translated to "justice on the grass",[9] took place in the communities effected by the genocide.]

We still don't know where some people were killed, although they were supposed to tell us where they had killed our families. I didn't get to meet the people who killed my family. I was young and since they were killed in a big group of people in the bushes, I couldn't personally identify who killed my family. Even though I don't know specifically who killed my parents, I have chosen to forgive them. I forgave them to release my heart. I used to think about the killers a lot, and when I saw people and would wonder if they were the ones who killed my family. To free myself, I have chosen to forgive them, even though I don't know them.

I became stronger when I went back to my home area of Bisesero

---

[9] http://www.preventgenocide.org/rw/amagambo2.htm

and went back to school. That's when I started having hope for the future. As I told you, I had felt that God had rejected us and I was angry with Him. After I got back to my home area and had to live there without a house and without food, I realized that God was the only one who cared. Because no one came to help, I was able to see the hand of God helping me. I changed my mindset about God, and I started to see that even though I was an orphan, God cared about me, protected me, and had me survive for a purpose. I knew there were many good people who were doing great things, and yet they were killed. I knew that there had to be a purpose and a reason why I wasn't killed during the genocide. Still now, I see how God cares for me. He's the only father I have, the only mother, and He is even like my brothers and sisters who died. Everything I have is from God.

Now I'm older and more mature, and I have hope for the future because Rwanda is safe. Even though I'm struggling to find a job, I have hope, because I have found different ways to survive. I pray that I will be able to go back to school, because I know this will lead to more opportunities for me.

I would like to teach people the importance of forgiveness, patience, love, unity, and reconciliation. I want to teach the importance of these elements of community because if communities follow them, genocide will not happen again.

Young people all over the world, I want you to know that you have power. You have the most assets for the economy of your country. If you use your power in a negative way, you will destroy your society. This is what happened in Rwanda in 1994. You need to know that even though you are young, you are important to your country and your community.

When people are told about what's happened in Rwanda, they need to make a choice to say, "Never again," not only in Rwanda, but all over the world. I would like my name to be included in this book, so that whoever reads this testimony can know it's told by a real person, and that this is not pretend. Thank you very much for reading this, and may God be with you.

[Innocent included the following Bible verse from Revelation 21:3-4 in his written narrative.]

"And I heard a loud voice from the throne saying, 'Look! God's dwelling place is now among the people, and he will dwell with them. They will be his people, and God himself will be with them and be their God. He will wipe every tear from their eyes. There will be no more death or mourning or crying or pain, for the old order of things has passed away...'"

IX: Alphonse Ngiriyeze

Name: Alphonse Ngiriyeze
Year and place of birth: 1983, Bisesero, Karongi District, Western Province
Age during genocide: eleven
Family members killed in genocide: mother, father, three siblings, many extended family members
Family members who survived genocide: few extended family members
Schooling completed: two years of university
Occupation: unemployed
Currently living with: lives alone
Language used for interview: written in Kinyarwanda and interpreted into English by Clement Ndayisaba

Before genocide my whole family lived in Bisesero. I had a mother, father, two brothers, and one sister. My parents were farmers, and we had four cows. We were Christians and attended a Pentecostal church. We lived in harmony with other Christians and we were at peace with our community.

I first learned of the ethnic groups in 1993. I heard people talking about the ethnic groups, and how some were better than others. People were singing songs about the Tutsis calling them *inyenzi* [cockroaches]. They talked about the RPF and called the leader of the RPF the chief of the *inyenzi*.

The genocide started on April 7, 1994. So many things changed so quickly. There were many people around that I didn't know, and no one knew whether they were coming or going. A group of people were moving past us, and when we asked where they were going and what they were doing they told us that they were coming to Bisesero because there was a lot of killing in their village. We learned the president had died, and that's why Tutsis were being killed. When the killers came to our home, we all ran. My parents went one way and my brother and I went another. On our journey, the killers found us and they killed my brother, so I was alone. After I saw my brother killed, I decided to try to go back home, but on my way back home I met the killers again. They didn't kill me, because they wanted me to take them back home and lead them to my parents. Midway there, they took me back to Bisesero. Miraculously they didn't kill me, and they decided to let me go. I went back home but I couldn't find anyone. After I got home and found no one, I decided to continue to move around the area, although I didn't know where my parents went. A short time later, I found out that my parents were also killed, as was my sister. I moved all around hiding in the bushes, and God protected me. Throughout the genocide I continued to hide and move around all the forests and bushes in Bisesero, and I know it was only God who protected me.

After the genocide I asked people if anyone from my family had survived, but no one survived. I asked how they killed my family, and I was told they first killed my parents, and then my brothers and my sister. My mother was killed two days before the French soldiers came to Bisesero. I only survived because I didn't stay with my parents, because they were killed while I had been with my older brother. Once I found out all my family was killed, I thought we had done something wrong that caused God to bring about all these terrible things.

After the genocide I went back to my home where we used to live, because I had nowhere to go. Our house had been destroyed and I had nowhere to live, so I lived with my neighbors and slept in different houses and places. I had many problems and challenges. I constantly thought about how I had lost my family and wondered what bad thing I had done to deserve this. I remembered and thought about them every day. After the genocide, I used to wrestle with God, and ask Him many questions. Are we true Christians? How could other people we go to church with be the killers? But even though I had questions, I realized that although my family had been killed, there must have been a reason for God to protect me and a purpose that He had for my life.

I survived alone. I have lost all of my immediate family. However, I have seen God working in my life in providing people to care for me even after my immediate family all died. Now I have realized that God has never left me. During the genocide, it was God who protected me against the killers. After genocide, I went back to live in Bisesero, and still live there now. Shortly after the genocide finished, I was taken by the RPF because there continued to be a lot of fighting in the area. They took us to Gitarama, and it was there I found other members of my extended family. After a short time in Gitarama, we were taken back to Bisesero and I tried to start school. I really struggled when I started school, because I didn't have a uniform or any school supplies. However, I was determined to finish my studies, and school helped me stay busy. When I look back on that time, I see that there were many lessons God taught me through the problems I was going through. I learned to change myself and to change other people. After genocide I fully dedicated my life to Jesus, because I learned that Jesus was the only one who would care for me, since my family was gone. He is the only one who sustains my life, provides for me, and He has given me the life I enjoy today.

There are still many consequences of the genocide. As a child, there was a group of us who would run around and play together. Now, I am one of the only people of my age group in my community, and that makes me sad. When my brother was killed and I was taken back to Bisesero, I was beaten along the way. I still have physical problems from being beaten by the killers. I still have back pain, and I'm not able to do much lifting. My family was not rich, but we had enough for our family. Today, the poverty I am living in is due to the genocide. I cannot pay for my school tuition and so I cannot finish university. There are days when I do not have enough money for food, and so I have to walk around to try to find someone who will give me some. In addition, I do not have my parents to help me make life decisions. In the past, I was so angry with those who had killed my family. I lived with a heavy sorrow, with wounds in my heart and intense pain in my body. There were many nights where I would not sleep. I felt like I could not trust anyone and was paranoid about people trying to hurt me or kill me.

I know the people who killed my father and older brother. However, I don't know who killed my mother or the other people in my family. I met the people who killed my father and brother during the Gacaca courts when they were sharing what had happened during the genocide. During Gacaca, people talked about the man who killed my father, who was still living in our community. Once people started talking about how he had killed, he immediately left the area, and no one knows where he is anymore. Some people say he moved to Kigali, but no one is sure where he is. They looked for him, but couldn't find him, although I know who he is. I have not seen him face to face since he left Bisesero. Even though he was not there, the Gacaca courts found the man who killed my father guilty, and if they find him he will serve time in prison and be punished.

I know the people who killed my brother, because I was with him when they killed him. He had taken me to a bush to hide me, and when he was looking for his own place to hide, they found him and killed him and left him there. After they finished killing him, they walked near my hiding spot in the bushes, and I saw their faces. There was a group of people who killed my brother, and some of them were taken to prison during Gacaca. One of them ran away and no one knows where he is or where he went. When I first met them I was very angry, and I didn't know if we could live in the same community again.

Today, I have forgiven those who I know and who were caught. I still do not know who the people were who killed my mom, other brother, and sister. I want to see the people who killed my father and mother and siblings again, so that I can forgive them. God does not want me to get revenge or to hold anger in my heart, and so I want to forgive them. The Gacaca courts did a good job, despite all the challenges, problems, and lies. [The Gacaca courts relied on the integrity and honesty of individuals to confess their crimes and publicly ask for forgiveness. This did not always happen, as some defendants didn't have a fair trial, while others lied or remained silent due to fears of repercussions.[10,11]] Although some people ran away, some killers came to repent what they had done, and we got to forgive them. It was good for us to learn how our families were killed.

Currently, my prayer is that what happened in Rwanda would not ever happen again here, or anywhere in the world. When I thought about God after the genocide, at first I was angry and upset with Him. After that, I was able to work through my emotions, and to dedicate my life to God and be baptized in the church. Today I have a good relationship with God, because He's the only one who has provided for me. I know God is faithful, and He is good. I have promised to stay near to God all my life. I always try to love others like I love myself, even when it is difficult.

The most important lesson I want people to learn from my life is to forgive others as Jesus forgave us. Revenge is not the solution in any situation, no matter what someone else has done to you. The

[10] https://www.un.org/en/preventgenocide/rwanda/historical-background.shtml
[11] https://www.hrw.org/news/2014/03/28/rwanda-justice-after-genocide-20-years

first lesson is to forgive as we have been forgiven. We are all created in the image of God. Nowhere does it say one ethnicity is better than another. Together we are stronger than we are individually. We can only build our communities and our countries by working together. Whatever you can do on your own is nothing compared to what you can do with God. If you allow God to use you, and change your heart and way of doing, you will be a part of changing others' lives.

A message to the youth: Remove divisions. Whether they are ethnic groups, race, sex, religion, or otherwise. Whatever divisions you may have, especially [about] race, remove them. You are the people who are building nations and communities. When God created Adam, he didn't tell him that some of his children would be black or white, or Hutu or Tutsi, but He created him and blessed him to have children all around the world that would not be divided.

[Alphonse included the following Bible verse from 1 Corinthians 13:4-7 in his written narrative.]

"Love is patient, love is kind. It does not envy, it does not boast, it is not proud. It does not dishonor others, it is not self-seeking, it is not easily angered, it keeps no record of wrongs. Love does not delight in evil but rejoices with the truth. It always protects, always trusts, always hopes, always perseveres."

X: Fabian Mushimiyimana

Name: Fabian Mushimiyimana
Year and place of birth: 1984, Mubuga, Karongi District, Western Province
Age during the genocide: ten
Family members killed in genocide: five immediate family members
Family members who survived genocide: two immediate family members
Schooling completed: currently in university
Occupation: project coordinator for Good News International communities in Karongyi District
Currently living with: mother
Language used for interview: written in Kinyarwanda and interpreted into English by Clement Ndayisaba

There were eight people in my immediate family, and we were farmers and owned cows. As far back as I can remember, there was always mistrust among our neighbors. We never lived at peace with each other, and many times, the Hutu people in our area did bad things to my family. My family were Christians, and although we went to the same church as some of our neighbors, living together in the same community was a challenge. I first learned about the ethnic groups in 1990, which is when I realized that many children my age in my community were Hutu.

The genocide started on the seventh of April in 1994. That day, we left our house and went to stay with my grandma for three days. After three days had passed, my uncle came and told us that the mayor of the sector had a meeting and said that every Tutsi in the district should be killed. At the meeting, he said that even Tutsi babies who were in their mothers' wombs should be killed. That evening, eight of my cousins were killed. We had to leave the home, and we went to hide in the bushes. It was raining so heavily that around 4:00 a.m., we decided to go to someone's house that was near where we were hiding. By chance, we ended up staying with this man in his house for two weeks. The killers didn't know where we were during those two weeks, but eventually they found out we were there and came to kill us. Before they entered the house, the people who we were living with had taken us to different places to hide us. They had already hidden me, but before they could get back to the house to hide the rest of my family the killers arrived and found them there. They immediately killed five members of my family, including my father. I was in the bush, and so I didn't know they had been killed or where they were. After they had hidden me there, I moved from house to house, and because I was no longer with my family, it was difficult for the killers to identify if I was Hutu or Tutsi. This is how I survived until the end of the genocide. During this time, I thought there was no God. I thought that what I had been taught about God was lies. I believed that if God really existed, we would not have been killed and I wouldn't be living such a horrible life.

After the genocide ended, I learned how my family was killed. There was nothing I could do. I felt helpless, angry, and full of grief for a long time. I stayed angry until the government pushed people to meet with the killers [and] for the killers to share what they had done. I know the people who killed my family; my mother told me who they were. She knew them because she saw them killing my family. I met them face to face. When I met them for the first time, they wanted to greet me, but I did not allow them to greet me as they wanted. I didn't trust them, and I thought they were going to do bad things to me again. As time went on, I have learned that what they did was the devil in them. God allowed me to see that they have changed, and I have started a new relationship with them by the power of God. I think the Gacaca courts were very helpful in that process, because it allowed us to learn how our families were killed, and where their bodies were taken. This has allowed us to find their bodies and give them proper burials to honor them appropriately. Some people have learned the truth through the Gacaca courts, which they would not have otherwise known. While the Gacaca courts were happening, we were taught the history of Rwanda, and we learned how the ethnic groups were used as a weapon to destroy our country. We learned how we had been deceived. We started to try to live at peace with each other, although we still have a long way to go. We met with refugees coming back from Congo and began to try to rebuild our lives by cultivating [farming], and animal husbandry [raising farm animals]. Some people have been able to forgive, but others have not.

Today, God gives me hope for the future, although there are still many consequences of the genocide. First is to live without family and to have lost our friends. There are times when we are grieving for those who have died, and we struggle living in poverty. Also, there is still some mistrust among people.

Our hope from the future cannot come from anyone but God. We believe that God is the only one who has cared for us and allowed us to live. I now have hope in God, and believe He's preparing a better future for me and for my family.

There are some lessons I want to teach others. One of the lessons is to tell people to fight against genocide and its ideology in Rwanda and all over the world so it will not happen again. We need to fight against anger and hate early, before people start killing one another. Another lesson is to know that divisions never build, they only destroy. Once you are united, you build and give a better future to your society. I wish that whoever reads this testimony will know that even though all this happened in Rwanda, the Rwanda of today is very different because of where God is taking this country. It's an amazing place and God is preparing a better future for all Rwandans. Thank you very much.

AFTERWORD

Forgiveness. Faith. Freedom. How could these themes persist in the narratives of survivors who had witnessed one of the most brutal genocides in history? How can a person choose to extend forgiveness to the people who used machetes to ruthlessly murder their loved ones? How can a person choose to maintain faith in a protecting God after being physically tortured? How can a person choose to live in freedom when the people who hunted them also walk freely within their communities?

Comprehending the genocide of the Tutsi in Rwanda challenged my own understanding of an omnipotent and omnipresent God. My faith in the God I experienced left me questioning how a loving and powerful God could allow such evil to occur to those who put their trust in Him. How could the God who said, "Let the little children come to me" (Matthew 19:14) allow these little children to suffer in unthinkable ways? No one and nothing could restore innocence to these traumatized souls. Young children were eyewitnesses to unimaginable acts of violence. Their pure bodies contracted diseases and were maimed and raped, resulting in excruciating mental, emotional, and physical suffering. Their formerly untainted ears continually heard the tormented screams of loved ones, as they agonizingly died in the depths of pit latrines. Their trusting hearts were shattered as former friends and neighbors murdered their loved ones. Their delicate spirits were crushed by the weight of trauma and crippling poverty. Many orphans struggled to provide themselves with the basics needed for physical survival.

A common theme that emerged among interviewees was a feeling of amazement when they initially met other survivors. In light of the mass murder they had witnessed they were incredulous to find other Tutsis who had also survived. Many people shared their feelings of survivor's remorse; surely death would have been more merciful in comparison to the life they now faced. Nothing could alleviate the memories that permeated their pasts and haunted their futures while a life of poverty and living alone stacked more odds against these young survivors.

Their commitment to the continuation of life captivated me. How was life in the wake of such death possible? How could orphans with mental, emotional, and physical scars have the capacity to build a future? I sought to unlock the lessons these young survivors had to teach. I was driven to seek answers and to understand such faith.

What I encountered in the aftermath of the genocide is seemingly incomprehensible, but what I learned and heard was validated in the way survivors lived in the aftermath, with unyielding faith and love for their neighbors. The strength it takes to kill is small in comparison with the strength it takes to lovingly embrace a killer. Although evil runs rampant in our world, when met with goodness, it's paralyzed. The impact of forgiveness extended by Rwandan survivors surpassed the destruction wrought by the killers. Their forgiveness set their own souls free.

Days once filled with death and despair are now lit with new life, with hope. The darkest forces of evil were at work in the destruction of Rwanda, but rebuilding and unifying the country through forgiveness was humanly impossible. The necessity to overcome evil created a situation in which the intervention of a loving God was essential for life to continue.

These narratives teach us to remember the pain of our Rwandan brothers and sisters in the years that have followed the genocide of 1994, and to remember the blessings of the lives of our own friends and family members. For some, these narratives are reminders of the pain we carry and the scars we bear. They are reminders of the loved ones we have lost and of the injustices we have suffered. Hearing the voices of Rwandan survivors allows us to identify with them through the traumatic experiences and losses within our own lives. Through these narratives we are given the ability to see the hope they have, and to find the hope we need to wake up to a new day. We have the opportunity to see the resilience required to keep on living after facing death. Through their strength we, too, can find strength to continue living with hope in spite of our past and in light of our present. These narratives are to remind you that you are not alone in your suffering, you are not alone in your pain. It is in our darkest, deepest moments of despair that the permeating rays of love and hope have the strongest power. In the midst of our most excruciating pain and undeniable weakness, grace is sweetest.

By living free, faith-filled, and forgiving lives, these survivors defy all odds. They demonstrate that they actively possess the keys to survival and that their lives are full of purpose. These are the voices of the next generation—the voices of hope.

"We are hard pressed on every side, but not crushed; perplexed, but not in despair; persecuted, but not abandoned; struck down, but not destroyed...Therefore we do not lose heart. Though outwardly we are wasting away, yet inwardly we are being renewed day by day. For our light and momentary troubles are achieving for us an eternal glory that far outweighs them all. So we fix our eyes not on what is seen, but on what is unseen, since what is seen is temporary, but what is unseen is eternal."

2 Corinthians 4:8-9, 16-18

GOOD NEWS INTERNATIONAL

Due to the massive numbers of widows and orphans, Rwanda has not been able to adequately meet the needs of these vulnerable people. In response to the need around him, Pastor Ben Kayumba founded the nonprofit organization Good News International.

Good News International strives to meet the needs of their community members in urban and rural communities across Rwanda. The five core areas of service within Good News are counseling, youth programs, income-generating activities, housing projects, and sponsorship. Through these services survivors are taught skills to help them start and maintain income-generating projects to alleviate their socio-economic poverty. In addition, opportunities for spiritual and emotional healing are provided to community members. Although many years have passed since the tragic events of 1994, there are many survivors who have never shared their experiences of the genocide. As a result, many people still suffer from significant trauma. Good News seeks to restore faith and hope to survivors through spiritual teaching and encouragement.

The Rwandan prison system was unable to house the large

number of perpetrators involved in the mass murders in 1994. As a result, the country established Gacaca courts. These informal courts were held within communities and asked killers to come forward and confess their crimes to the surviving family members. Once confession and forgiveness occurred, many survivors and killers returned to live in the same communities. To address this issue of reunification, Good News started a community called Tubumwe, which means "we are one." This community is composed of perpetrators, survivors, inter-ethnic families, and those who returned to Rwanda after years of exile. The focus of this community is to truly achieve unity in a way that replaces generations of division to impact the next generation and thus change the future narrative of Rwanda.

For more information about Good News International and the work that is being done within communities across Rwanda, please visit https://www.goodnewsintl.org/.

Inshuti International is the American nonprofit partner to Good News International and is based in Milwaukee, Wisconsin. For more information on Inshuti International and opportunities for partnership, please visit http://www.inshuti-international.org.

ACKNOWLEDGEMENTS

Clement Ndayisaba interpreted the oral interviews and translated the written interviews. Clement is a staff member of Good News International and has relationships with all the people who were interviewed. Uniform translation and validation of personal information maintained the integrity of the narratives. Without Clement, none of this would have been possible. Clement, thank you for the hours you spent interpreting, answering my many questions without judgement, and for your unwavering patience with me and belief in me. I am deeply indebted to you for all you have done.